ANYWHERE

The Handbook for Digital Nomads, by Digital Nomads

Created by AND CO in Partnership
with 100+ Digital Nomads

HOW TO USE THIS GUIDE

This book reflects the collective wisdom of 100+ nomads and nomad experts. Since no two nomads' experiences will be the same, we suggest using these first-hand accounts as a starting point to your research. In addition to leaning on the advice of our contributors, we recommend using our Appendix (p. 144) to explore additional resources from trusted organizations who can provide more detailed information within more specific topics.

1: Making the Leap: The 70-20-10 Rule	13
2: Making the Transition to a Nomadic Lifestyle	21
3: Building Your Safety Net for Remote Work	31
4: How to Select Your Host City	43
5: Finding the Best Living Situation for You	53
6: The Ultimate Digital Nomad Packing List	65
7: The Digital Nomad's Tool Belt	77
8: Visas 101	83
9: How to Find Work as a Nomad	91
10: Effective Communications Strategies for Nomads	99
11: Setting Your Business Goals	107
12: Tax & Legal Watch-Outs for Digital Nomads	115
13: Starting a Nomad Family? Start Here	123
14: Wellness & Self-Care as a Nomad	129
15: How to Be a Student of the World	135
16: SOS! Emergency Numbers & Resources for Nomads	140
17: AND CO's Big List of Digital Nomad Resources	144

ABOUT AND CO

AND CO helps independent workers run their businesses from anywhere by providing tools such as multi-currency invoicing, automated expense-tracking and more. We believe in empowering the digital nomad movement by providing these professionals with the resources needed to focus on what they love: work and travel. AND CO is free to try. Get started at www.and.co/digital-nomads.

INTRODUCTION

The world feels a lot smaller these days. Technology has seeped into virtually every industry, widening the possibilities for remote work to more people than ever before. Fueled by freedom and ambitious in their expectations when it comes to how work and life should meet and intertwine, independent workers are pioneering location-agnostic career paths that are taking them, well, anywhere.

You might know them as digital nomads. Simply put, digital nomads are professionals who live and work remotely. Their jobs, either with a single employer or—more commonly—across several employers as independent workers, are inherently digital, which means their physical locations at a given moment are not tied to their ability to do their jobs. Digital nomads take full advantage of technology's capacity to dissolve borders to combine their passion for travel and exploration with their career ambitions. They are, indeed, a unique and growing group.

ANYWHERE

Nomadism is certainly not for everyone, but if you have an itch to explore and push the boundaries of a more traditional work lifestyle, then it might be something to pursue. In our recently published survey on the state of freelance, **The Slash Workers** (www.and.co/slash-workers), 60 percent of respondents told us they would be interested in exploring a nomadic lifestyle in the future. Of all freelancers we interviewed, a quarter of them were already living and working remotely. What's more, the digital nomads reported a better quality of life on average.

Of course, if you're not already living out the digital nomad fantasy, diving in can seem like a daunting prospect. Which cities or regions are the best fit for you? How will you find and maintain a solid pipeline? Do you need a visa? What about taxes? How do you handle income earned abroad? Where do you even begin?

We designed this book as a primer for anyone who is interested in making the leap to digital nomadism. We partnered with more than 100 digital nomads to curate the must-know tips and advice from the people who know best.

SO, ARE YOU READY TO TAKE YOUR TALENTS ANYWHERE?

Chapter 1

MAKING THE LEAP: THE 70-20-10 RULE

By Josh Hayford
◊ Denver, CO

Deciding to uproot yourself and embrace a nomadic lifestyle is a big decision, and actually making the leap is no small task. As you stand at the precipice of turning your dream into a reality, I'm here to help.

As someone who has mulled over becoming a digital nomad, and eventually making the move myself, I'm here to share my tried-and-true formula for overcoming beginner's paralysis. It's called the 70-20-10 Rule, and it follows that jumping into a nomadic lifestyle is 70 percent research, 20 percent preparation and 10 percent improvisation. Let's break it down.

ANYWHERE

70 PERCENT RESEARCH

I am the sort of person that never goes into anything unprepared. I mean, I can't even buy a toaster without spending hours poring over online reviews to make sure I'm getting the best product for my buck. When I decided to go the nomad route, it was the same way and as it turns out, my obsessive need to be informed helped me immensely. If you do your research ahead of time, you will drastically cut down on the number of surprises that are in store for you. (By the way, reading this book is a solid first step! Good on you.)

Research can help you figure out what kind of lifestyle you want to live. Some nomads prefer to plan an extended overseas trip, spanning months or even years. They travel light, and given the distances they traverse, they rack up a ton of airline miles. Other nomads move around but remain inland, renting a motorhome or RV (some even living out of a van) and opt to drive from destination to destination. Other nomads still prefer curated experiences, in which they join a group of fellow nomads as part of an organized, community-based effort that usually "docks" in one city.

CHAPTER 1

Of course, every option has perks and drawbacks. Leading a nomadic lifestyle is a delicate balance of comfort, cost and freedom—pick two. If you want freedom paired with comforts, expect to pay a premium. Want something a little more comfortable, but at a lower cost? Your budget might not allow you to move as often, cutting into your freedom. The dizzying array of options and ways to balance these three qualities can be extremely overwhelming.

The key is finding out what will work for you. Whatever style of travel interests you, scour the forums related to it. Read everything you can find, and take notes if you need help organizing your thoughts. Do yourself a favor and focus on the bad stuff. Yep! I am asking you to be pessimistic for a moment.

There are forums and websites full of posts and comments from people who made an attempt at this lifestyle and decided it wasn't for them. Read their stories and hear them out. Put yourself in their shoes and honestly ask yourself, "How would these problems affect me?" Chances are, you will find yourself modifying your plans based on the experiences of others, both good and bad.

A critical piece of the research phase is establishing a realistic budget. No matter how you embrace this lifestyle, it's going to cost you something. You can live a nomadic lifestyle on a fixed budget, of course, but if you're careless your new lifestyle can get very expensive very quickly. Carefully research the costs involved, and include everything that you might possibly need on the road. Food, fuel (if you're driving), transportation costs (if you're getting around that way), insurance, club memberships, entertainment, internet—just to name a few—must all be considered.

NOMAD TIP:

"Digital nomadism is at times chaotic, stressful, and difficult, like any job, and it can be easy to romanticize it. You have the freedom to move wherever you want, but make no mistake about it, it's still a job and all the pressures, stresses, and occasional mundane aspects that creep into any job will still be there."

Joseph Engelmajer, Web Developer
Bali, Indonesia

CHAPTER 1

> "CHANCES ARE, YOU WILL FIND YOURSELF MODIFYING YOUR PLANS BASED ON THE EXPERIENCES OF OTHERS, BOTH GOOD AND BAD."

When it comes to researching the various paths you may take, keep in mind that someone else has already been there and done that. Learn from their mistakes and emulate their triumphs. Optimize their experiences to suit your own goals and lifestyle needs. Stand on the shoulders of those who have gone before, and your path will be that much easier.

20 PERCENT PREPARATION

So, now you know what to expect and you're ready to face the triumphs (and the pitfalls, too!) that come with it. It's time to apply what you've learned and start preparing for your new life. Preparation will be different for every person, depending on what your research has led you to decide, but here are some general best practices for you to consider.

For most people, the hardest part of the hardest part of becoming a digital nomad is cutting ties with their former "stationary" lives. If you own a home, selling it can often be the biggest hurdle. Perhaps you rent and need to break a lease—that can be difficult, too. Deciding which possessions you can take with you and which must be sold or placed in storage is yet another step that can be physically and emotionally draining. If you have a traditional job, you'll need to give notice and plan your departure. And of course, saying farewell (albeit temporarily) to loved ones can be the hardest step of all.

ANYWHERE

As you tie up loose ends and bid farewell to your former life, you'll need to concurrently prepare for your new life. This involves buying the things you'll need, updating insurance companies and sorting out residency and mail issues. If you have health care needs, you need to determine how you'll meet them while abroad or on the road. You should also consider joining clubs that will help you along the way. For example, for mobile nomads there are several roadside assistance companies that offer discounts at hotels and RV parks. International nomads might seek out local meetups or communities of nomads in the areas they intend to live. Depending on how you choose to travel, you might sign up for one or a dozen.

The good news is that if you've done your research, this should be the easiest step. You should know exactly what you need to do, and what equipment you'll need to make a nomadic life feasible. This is also the most exciting step, because you can finally see the fruits of all your research paying off. You're about to start your new journey, and it's so close you can almost reach out and touch it.

10 PERCENT IMPROVISATION
This is the final phase, and it never really ends. While research and preparation will minimize the number of unpleasant surprises you encounter, no matter how much research you do or how well you prepare, you're going to run into something that you don't quite know how to handle. This could be anything from issues with internet connectivity to challenges getting around a new remote city. It could even involve an illness or injury, far from home and your preferred doctor.

Being able to think on your feet and roll with whatever comes your way is a requirement for leading a nomadic lifestyle. Encountering a show-stopping issue can be scary—particularly if it seems like it might be very expensive to solve, or if it involves your health or wellbeing. The key is to remain calm and focus on solutions, not problems. I'm a firm believer that where there's a will, there's a way; you just need to match your willpower to the task at hand.

Finally, remember being "independent," doesn't necessarily mean being alone. Don't be afraid to rely on fellow wanderers. The people I've run into while living as a nomad have been the kindest, most helpful folks I've ever met, and if you take to the internet you'll find thousands of friendly, helpful people just waiting to offer up their wisdom at a moment's notice.

On a personal note, making the leap into a nomadic lifestyle has been the most freeing, happiest, and scariest experience of my life. I wouldn't trade it for anything—and I believe that if you approach it with the right attitude, and follow this guide, you won't want to give it up, either.

ABOUT THE AUTHOR

Born and raised amid the Green Mountains of Vermont, Josh Hayford has been a digital nomad since 2016. Programmer, writer, musician, gamer, beer lover and dog enthusiast, he manages to squeeze a full career and a complete complement of hobbies into a 38-foot motorhome.

✉ jshayford@gmail.com

Chapter 2

MAKING THE TRANSITION TO A NOMADIC LIFESTYLE

By Romina Viola
◊ New York, NY

There's a lot more to a nomadic lifestyle than cool Instagram pictures and working from quaint cafés around the world. Despite living in constantly changing locales, from luxurious to exotic, nomads know that the work goes hand-in-hand with the lifestyle. So, if you're ready to make a move—and ready to build your career from anywhere, as the title of this book suggests—the next step is to think about how you plan to transition into a full-time nomadic lifestyle.

ANYWHERE

WHAT DOES IT MEAN TO BE A DIGITAL NOMAD?

A nomad is a member of a community that travels, moving from a place to another, in order to sustain their basic needs. "Nomad" is a word from a world and a culture that was here way before us, before the internet and before civilization as we know it today.

For that reason, it's necessary to re-define the term "nomad" in the context of today's digital nomad movement. Digital nomads are not driven by necessity, fleeing the elements or chasing the promise of another region. Conversely, digital nomads are motivated by freedom and an inner urge for exploration and discovery.

The BBC defines "digital nomad" as a person who "relies on digital telecommunications and the internet to make a living." While these individuals could access the internet from their hometown, they have decided to quit the concept of "home" in its singular context and forge a life of transience and travel. Instead of chasing their living, as was the case with traditional nomads, they are chasing something else. What will you chase as a nomad? Experiences, memories, perspectives and new ways to see the world.

> "DIGITAL NOMADS ARE MOTIVATED BY FREEDOM AND AN INNER URGE FOR EXPLORATION AND DISCOVERY."

CHAPTER 2

TRANSITIONING YOUR CAREER

This is where you start. If your current job doesn't allow remote working, you'll need to find a new job. You'll also need to work on your personal brand. You need to create a great resume that can define you better than a first-person interview can. Work on your portfolio, talk to old colleagues, and network your way into the position you want.

You'll be able to dig up thousands of posts online about finding a full-time remote position or about performing contract work remotely across one or many clients. Many job boards (such as **Dribbble** and **AngelList**) include built-in search functionality for remote positions. There are also several lists of fully-remote companies like Zapier, Invision and Buffer that are hiring on an ongoing basis. If you prefer contract-based work across several partners, you'll want to communicate your move with clients well in advance.

In any case, it's important to have a full-time remote opportunity or contract work lined up (with a healthy pipeline!) well ahead of packing your bags to move. The process of scouring job boards, lining up interviews and kicking off projects will undoubtedly become much harder once you move. Perhaps the most important step in your preparation should be to ensure you have a steady pipeline of work to sustain you while you're away from home.

STORE OR SHED YOUR MATERIAL POSSESSIONS

Organizational consultant Marie Kondo would have a lot to say about this next section, but perhaps a good starting point is writing down the title of her book: **"The Life-Changing Magic of Tidying Up: The Japanese Art of Decluttering and Organizing"** (available on Amazon). Kondo's book has ushered a decluttering movement that is, quite appropriately, growing in parallel to the rise of digital nomadism. Indeed, aspiring nomads have much to learn from her best practices for living a more minimalistic existence.

NOMAD TIP:

"Donate all the items you won't be bringing with you. Keeping them in storage is useless. I have a box of things at a family member's basement back in the States and I don't miss anything in there. As soon as I return, I'll be getting rid of it all."

Sara Nourse, Content Creator
Greece

CHAPTER 2

TOP TIPS FOR A MINIMAL LIFESTYLE

1. **Pile and purge:** Gather all of your items in one heap, and then remove items one at a time and make the decision to lose or keep.
2. **If you don't love it, lose it:** Chances are, if you have to think twice about keeping an item, you really don't need it after all.
3. **Let go of nostalgia:** We all have items with sentimental value, but not everything we own needs to be tied to a memory. Your memories are your memories, and they live in your mind, not in your belongings. Let go.
4. **Respect your stuff:** With fewer possessions, you'll learn to treat them better. That new shawl? Maybe not best stored in a ball at the bottom of your suitcase.
5. **Learn the art of the fold:** Kondo points out that folding is a lot more space-efficient than hanging. Folded clothes are also much easier to transport!

Credit: Marie Kondo

ANYWHERE

In Kondo's words, "You don't need more space; you need less stuff." So, let's start with physical things. As a nomad, you'll have to be able to pack your entire routine and sometimes, apartment, into a backpack or suitcase (and sometimes that suitcase is a carry-on!). Being nomadic, therefore being relatively portable, means leaving behind the comfort of your home to embark on a trip during which you'll encounter several homes with varying degrees of comfort and familiarity.

For this there's really only one best practice: Bring with you only what you really need. Moving around with heavy luggage is very expensive and inconvenient. As someone who prioritizes exploration and adventure over "things," going minimal will be a manageable exercise. Promise.

TIPS FOR MANAGING THE CHAOS

Something you will learn as soon as you hit the road is that you cannot enjoy a new city if you procrastinate the same way you did in your grey office back home.

If your remote gig doesn't mandate that you clock-in during set hours, a good rule of thumb is to divide your day in blocks (called "time-blocking"). Choose the activities you want to fulfill during your day, and make sure you leave enough "blocks" of hours during the day to complete your projects with the right amount of focus and participate in your employer's preferred communication channels.

Remember: Nomadic doesn't equal chaotic. Organization is key. Underline this, bookmark it and write it in your notebook. Lacking the right organizational tools and mindset, you risk losing precious time in a beautiful, foreign city. Make the most of your work hours to make the most of your leisure time.

CHAPTER 2

"MAKE THE MOST OF YOUR WORK HOURS TO MAKE THE MOST OF YOUR LEISURE TIME."

On the subject of leisure time, here's something else to keep in mind as you transition to a nomadic lifestyle, and that's the change in social relationships. As you say your goodbyes to friends back home, you might question your decision or feel anxious about the prospect of re-constructing your social web. But as you spend time away, though you'll miss your friends and family–sometimes terribly so–you will get the opportunity to make new connections every single day. The commonly-held drive among nomads can be a source of community. In a co-working space, for example, you'll likely meet other professionals who share similar experiences as you. You can join virtual or IRL communities of freelancers or remote workers in the city you're visiting. Some people organize meet ups wherever they go, from professional fireside chats to bar crawls with dozens of people from countries around the world.

Digital nomadism is a new and perfect opportunity to connect with the world. You'll find how much the word "friend" can stretch to fit in all this new people you've just met yet feel so familiar to you.

ANYWHERE

CREATING YOUR GAME-PLAN

Now that we have taken a closer look at the nomadic lifestyle, it's time to ask yourself a series of questions that will determine the next steps to follow. Let's kick off with the dreaded budget plan.

> **"LET GO, OPEN UP, AND YOU'LL BE WELL ON YOUR WAY."**

Your budget plan begins with a series of choices. To finish this chapter, let's review some of these questions to ask yourself. The answers will lead to several conditions to keep in mind if you intend to embrace a nomadic lifestyle.

- **About the work:** Will you work remotely for the same company you work for today? Will you find a remote position? Will you quit your job and freelance? Will you start your own brand on the road?
- **About the company:** Will you travel alone or are you joining a nomadic group? Is there someone in your life you'll be bringing with you? Are you more comfortable pursuing a curated experience, which might charge a premium?
- **About your destination:** Will you stay in the same place for a long period (one to three months)? Will you stay less than a months in a single place before packing your bags and heading to the next destination? Which destinations will you prioritize first? How will you get around?
- **About your budget and bureaucracy:** What do you expect to spend during one month away? What passport do you currently have and what visas do you need? Will you work from your accommodation? Will you find a co-working space? Do you have or need travel insurance?

CHAPTER 2

If you take away one insight from this chapter, let it be this: Transitioning from your current lifestyle to that of a nomad is about learning to let go of the things (namely, material possessions) you do not need, and opening yourself up to the experiences that will define your life as a nomad.

ABOUT THE AUTHOR

Romina Viola has a degree in Social Communication but has always worked in digital marketing. She might become a journalist some day. Right now, she loves writing, cooking and traveling. A full-time digital nomad from Argentina, you can find her in a kitchen, at a concert or behind her computer.

 @romikid

 @romikid

 www.kiloindiadelta.com

Chapter 3

BUILDING YOUR SAFETY NET FOR REMOTE WORK

By Ashley Nowicki, Founder of Auctor (Latin for Pioneer)
San Francisco, CA

The key to making the leap into the nomadic lifestyle is courage, first and foremost, but there are a series of steps you can take to build up that courage. The easiest path for a fearless transition into a nomadic lifestyle is to create an established safety net, so if you stumble or fall, you'll be able to get right back on your feet. What do I mean by that? Keep reading.

STEP #1: CHECK-UP FROM THE NECK UP

The first order of business is to take stock of your mental health. Going nomadic is thrilling, but it will also test many parts of you. Many nomads have praised the benefit of daily meditation (made super-simple with apps like **Headspace**) when it comes to preparing for and managing the mental and emotional rigors of life on the road. Be ready to interact with strangers regularly and embrace the adventure that comes with being lost in foreign places.

Another quick tip? Save some room in your suitcase for a couple of small items that make you feel at home no matter where you are: your favorite slippers, a Bluetooth speaker, your favorite thermos, etc. These will help when symptoms of homesickness strike.

> "SAVE SOME ROOM IN YOUR SUITCASE FOR A COUPLE OF SMALL ITEMS THAT MAKE YOU FEEL AT HOME NO MATTER WHERE YOU ARE."

Oh, and stock up on reading materials in advance because they will come in handy when dining solo, which can be one of the loneliest parts of nomadic life. Audiobooks and podcasts are great for delayed flights and long trains. **Pocket** (www.getpocket.com) will help you stash all of those articles and tweets into a sleek content stream that you can conjure up later on.

STEP #2: CRUNCH THE NUMBERS

Now, it's time to dive into the finances. Building your financial safety net will be the most stressful part about going nomadic, so it's best to attack this step head-on. Your financial security system will look different depending on who you are and where you're going (as well as for how long you plan to stay), but there are a handful of common denominators to get you started.

First, start with your skill set. What you do for a living, and how established you are in that career, will greatly influence the type of financial safety net you need to build. Skill sets like software engineering, writing, product design, visual design and recruitment can be done from most anywhere. On the flip side, roles in management or human resources are more likely to require an onsite presence and may be harder to secure remotely.

Next, be honest with yourself about your seniority. Charging too much for your experience may prevent companies from booking you. Director-level roles may be more difficult to secure remotely because you are expected to lead a team day in, day out. That said, charging too little may also disservice you because you may end up having to take on multiple projects at once to make up for charging a lower rate, forcing you to work longer hours and juggle more expectations. It's also important to keep in mind that the rate you set on Day 1 will likely hold, so if the work becomes recurring, you'll be stuck in that rate.

NOMAD TIP:

"Charge what you are worth. Just because you do not have overhead and can work anywhere doesn't mean you should charge less than people who have an office. I have much better clients who are willing to pay for my services now that I am charging the correct prices."

Rose Lawless, International Researcher
Palm Beach, Florida

CHAPTER 3

For those just starting out in their career, factor in being newer to the game and stay focused on opportunities that will create credibility for you in the space, especially as a remote team member. For those who are more senior, consider whether leading a team or staying close to the work matters more to you.

To figure out your rate, there are two different but equally effective, equations to use as a starting point.

Both start with your ideal annual salary. Keep in mind that currency conversions and the cost of living abroad will constantly fluctuate, so plan accordingly. AND CO just launched the ability to create expenses, income and invoices in any currency, which is another great way to stay on top of this.

ANYWHERE

OPTION ONE: BY DAY

Calculate your freelance rate by taking your annual salary and dividing it by 260. This is the average number of working days in a calendar year.

Example: $130,000 USD / 260 = $500 per day

The result is the amount you'd have to charge per workday to reach your ideal number, if you worked every work day of the year. However, this doesn't factor in time off for travel or for time between bookings. To address both of these parameters, consider dividing your ideal annual income by 230. Some of you will take more than 30 days off in a year, some of you may take less. Adjust accordingly based on your personal preferences.

Example: $130,000 USD / 200 (factoring in two months off) = $650 per day

OPTION TWO: BY HOUR

Again, start with your ideal annual salary. Take that number and divide by 2,080. This is the number of working hours in a year without any holidays factored in.

Example: $130,000 / 2,080 = $62.50 per hour

Multiply the quotient by 25 percent, add it to the quotient and the sum is your target hourly rate. Adjust your rate up to factor in days off for the calendar year as needed.

Example: $62.50 x 25% = $15.63 (rounded to $15.50)

Example: $62.50 + $15.50 = $78 (rounded up) = $80 per hour

One very important thing to remember is that neither of these equations factor in the money you will need to set aside to pay taxes. Many accountants in the U.S. recommend setting a third of your income aside for taxes (roughly 34 percent). If you're financially conservative, you might even set 40 to 50 percent aside to be safe.

Since your income places you in one of several tax brackets, keep in mind that the higher the day rate, the more you'll need to stash for taxes. This percentage will also depend on your country of origin, so do your research or hop on the phone with your accountant to talk through the best plan of action for you.

The final step in building this financial safety net is to start saving. Think about how much money you'll need to be financially sound for at least three months and build your savings account accordingly. That way, if you hit a dry patch with projects or decide to take extra time off, you won't be stressed.

STEP #3: RESPECT YOUR HEALTH

Dealing with doctors overseas can be easy or difficult, depending on what part of the world you're traveling in. A good rule of thumb is to get all preventative health check-ins done, and on your local health insurance, before you leave. Before heading out, you'll also want to check in with your local insurance provider to see if they offer coverage overseas. Even if you do have international insurance, most foreign medical providers will request payment upfront at the time of service, so save all your receipts so you can be accurately reimbursed by your provider.

NOMAD TIP:

"It's going to be a lot more expensive than you think. Get savvy with flights and accomodations while traveling and eat breakfast and lunch at your apartment so you can have more money to put toward weekend getaways. Try to save as much as possible before you hit the road."

Allison Ward, PR Specialist
Medellin, Colombia

CHAPTER 3

"GET ALL PREVENTATIVE HEALTH CHECK-INS DONE, AND ON YOUR LOCAL HEALTH INSURANCE, BEFORE YOU LEAVE."

I also recommend adding travel insurance when booking your flight to cover potential unforeseen medical needs. **The U.S. Department of State** provides a list of medical insurance providers for overseas coverage at www.travel.state.gov.

Keep in mind that some countries require specific vaccinations upon entry so you may need to plan accordingly, depending on where you're traveling. You typically need to see a healthcare professional four to six weeks before international travel to receive any vaccinations. Head to the **Center for Disease Control** Travelers Health website (wwwnc.cdc.gov/travel) for specifics listed by country.

STEP #4: STAY CONNECTED

You may not know where you're going to be three months from now, but you most likely know where you'll be in three weeks time. Call your cell phone carrier and find out how much it costs to roam in that country. If it's more than $7/day, consider other options.

My Webspot (www.my-webspot.com) offers unlimited pocket Wi-Fi globally and prices range depending on the country (max is ~$10/day). This service allows you to make calls over Skype, WhatsApp FaceTime, Viber, and Google Hangout while also allowing you to do work from anywhere by setting up a remote hotspot. They'll also deliver your device to your hotel or Airbnb address and offer airport pickup at most of the larger international airports. If delivered, a return envelope is provided so all you have to do is drop it in a local post box.

ANYWHERE

Another option is to pick up a local SIM card for your phone, allowing you to utilize your phone like you're a local. One caveat here: Your cell phone number will change, so keep this mind when dealing with clients remotely. It may be a pain to update your team every couple of weeks with a new contact number if you are bouncing between countries, but if you're staying in one country for an extended period of time, it's a solid solution.

Finally, make sure you always filter for Wi-Fi when booking accommodations to save yourself any potential headaches upon arrival.

STEP #5: STAY ORGANIZED

There are a handful of apps and tools available that will help bring structure and balance to your flexible nomadic lifestyle. Below are some favorites, and for a complete list check out AND CO's Big List of Digital Nomad Resources on pg. 144.

- **Headspace:** Meditation you can do when you want, wherever you are, in just ten minutes a day.
- **Trello:** Project management tool that allows you to track progress with your team from anywhere.
- **Google Translate:** Translate text, voice, images and more. Download it for offline use in remote areas without Wi-Fi access.
- **Hotel Tonight:** Find discounted hotel accommodations up to seven days in advance.
- **ClassPass:** A monthly membership that allows you to visit different workout studios across the U.S. and in cities like London, Vancouver, Sydney, Melbourne, Brisbane and others.
- **Audible:** Includes more than 215,000 audio books and programs for your listening pleasure that can also be downloaded for offline use.

CHAPTER 3

Take the time to do a bit of preparation before hitting the road. It will pay off in both the short run and the long run, making your experience much more enjoyable.

Note: The author of this article is not a certified public accountant. The article was produced for informational purposes only and should not be substituted for the advice of an accountant.

ABOUT THE AUTHOR

Ashley is the Founder of Auctor, an exclusive collective fostering new ventures for world-class artists, engineers, product designers, filmmakers and more. She is also the creator of L A N D S C A P E, a bi-monthly publication showcasing companies working across social, cultural, technological and scientific tensions with an impressive creative twist. In her spare time, Ashley writes code and travels the world as a digital nomad.

 @wickiiwickii

 www.latinforpioneer.io

Chapter 4

HOW TO SELECT YOUR HOST CITY

By Lauren M. Alexander
⚲ Merida, Mexico

Being a digital nomad offers the kind of freedom and flexibility that most people never dreamed possible. Trading in the 9-to-5 grind and morning commute to be able to move freely around the world and work at your own pace? Yes, please!

But first—where will you go? Choosing a host city is one of the most important decisions you'll make as a digital nomad, and there are several important factors to consider before booking your next flight to realize your location-independent dreams. This chapter outlines a few important considerations to keep in mind as you plan your epic nomadic experience.

ANYWHERE

DOES THE LOCALE HAVE A NOMAD COMMUNITY?

Nestling into a city that has a vibrant community of digital nomads will no doubt lead to a more secure and enjoyable experience. If socializing with fellow nomads and meeting like-minded professionals is "up there" on your list, then you'll want to make sure that the cities you vet are nomad-friendly.

Cities like Chiang-Mai, Medellin and Berlin are flourishing with digital nomads, and a quick Google search reveals many more international destinations sorted by popularity. **Nomad List** (www.nomadlist.io), founded by nomad pioneer Pieter Levels, is widely heralded as the top resource for vetting a city's nomad potential.

Being in a city with other nomads will offer you a built-in network of open individuals who can help familiarize you with the culture, and of course to introduce you to all the hot spots around town. If the community aspect is important to you, make sure you check this box first before going any further in your planning efforts. Similarly, if your aim is to get off the beaten path entirely, take this into consideration as you research potential host cities.

CHAPTER 4

ARE THERE CO-WORKING SPACES APLENTY?

Co-working spaces, a natural by-product of a strong nomad presence, are key for those who thrive within the structure of an office-like environment but still appreciate the freedom to come and go as they please.

Sharing space with others who are also on-the-grind can help you stay on track throughout the day during those moments when you'd rather turn on the TV or take an after lunch siesta. Taking a break to socialize can help increase productivity in the long run and can lead to more creative ideas and solutions in your work.

Established nomad hubs will no doubt have co-working spaces aplenty, and tools like **ShareDesk** (www.sharedesk.net) make it easy to browse by region. Another resource to bookmark is **Workfrom** (www.workfrom.co). Workfrom provides an up-to-date database of coffee shops, cafes and co-working offices across 1,250 cities worldwide. The resource is curated by 2,000 nomad contributors, so you can be sure you're always uncovering the most reliable, nomad-friendly locations no matter where your travels may take you.

WHAT'S THE WI-FI SITUATION?

Wi-Fi is a digital nomad's lifeline. Being a productive digital nomad necessitates that you have a strong and consistent connection to the rest of the world. When you are working hundreds, if not thousands, of miles away from your team and employer, it's imperative to have access to a steady connection at all times.

ANYWHERE

While places that are off-the grid may seem appealing at first, if you're not able to effectively work from your laptop, the trade-off is probably not worth it in the long run. There are of course exceptions to this rule: For example, if you're hard at work on the next great American novel or plugging away on a screenplay, perhaps the lack of distractions could work to your advantage.

ARE THERE SAFE AND AFFORDABLE RENTALS?

For many nomads, couch-surfing and hostel-hopping aren't going to cut it. Settling down somewhere for a month at the very least is critical to avoid travel burnout and to maintain productivity in the long term. For this reason, safe and affordable housing is an absolute must.

For the cheapest rentals, it's best to conduct a search in the native language of your host country to avoid hiked-up tourist prices. It may also help to have a local by your side to make sure you're in a safe location, and to negotiate with the landlord to make sure you're getting the best deal. Month-to month pre-furnished rentals are ideal, and proximity to public transportation and restaurants and cafes can be added perks. For a solid listing of long term rentals, check out **Long Term Lettings** (www.longtermlettings.com).

IS THE CITY CLOSE TO OTHER AREAS OF INTEREST?

If you're stationed somewhere for more than a few months, chances are you'll want to explore areas outside of your selected city. You may not always have the time or the money to hop on a flight to go somewhere new on a whim, so selecting a location that is within a reasonable distance to other destinations by car, bus or train is a huge plus.

NOMAD TIP:
"I spent my first two years as a digital nomad working alone from cafes, not realizing there were entire communities of people like me working out of coworking spaces. They are a great way to meet awesome new people and increase your productivity."

Leanne Beesley, co-founder, Coworker.com
Spain

ANYWHERE

ARE THERE WEATHER EXTREMES?

Choosing a place that is neither too hot nor too cold is essential to be able to move around comfortably. Because you're not on vacation and can't escape the sweltering heat or the frigid cold and run back home to safety, making sure the climate in your host city agrees with you is pretty much a non-negotiable.

Being able to go outside for walks to clear your mind, exploring the city at your leisure, and being outside in nature are just a few things that will allow you to live somewhere longer than your average backpacker. You are ultimately the one who decides what works (and doesn't work) for you climate-wise, so make sure to read up on average yearly temperatures and weather patterns so you're not in for any surprises.

IS THERE FRIENDLY LOCAL CULTURE?

Arguably one of the most rewarding aspects of travel is being able to experience the local culture and connect with people who live there. Even if you don't speak the native language, a friendly smile or a head-nod is sometimes all you need to feel welcome and safe in your host country.

Developing a relationship with the locals is not only a great way to learn the language, but it also allows you to experience nuances and everyday aspects of their culture that may not be visible to travelers or other digital nomads. Having a local community that is somewhat integrated with the expat or nomadic community makes for a friendlier, more dynamic, and less "us vs. them" experience overall.

CHAPTER 4

At the end of the day, your criteria for selecting a host city will be personal and unique to your business and particular goals. The most important thing is that you actually want to be where you are going. So, make sure you don't choose your destination based solely on a checklist, but allow it to be a balance between the things need to get by, and the things that reflect your personal tastes.

ABOUT THE AUTHOR

Lauren Alexander is a freelance writer currently based in Merida, Mexico. She left her job as a staff writer for an agricultural publication in July 2015 craving the freedom offered by a location-independent lifestyle. She eventually found her way to the sunny Yucatan Peninsula where she has been traveling, learning, and expanding ever since.

 @lamarialex

 www.jophielle.co

10 TRENDING NOMAD CITIES

If you need a little inspiration as you set your sights on a nomadic life, begin your search with these ten trending cities for remote workers. Each boast a Nomad Score™ of 100% on Nomad List, proving that they are ideal spots to live out your work and personal dreams.

1. CHIANG MAI, THAILAND
Chiang Mai, or the "rose of the North," is Thailand's largest northern city that boasts a more mountainous, calming alternative to the hustle and bustle of Bangkok. It still retains vestiges of the Old City with monasteries, barefoot monks, and a plethora of history, but has now turned into an urban hub that's ripe for digital nomads.

2. LISBON, PORTUGAL
Lisbon is one of the friendliest places you'll ever visit. A truly illuminated city, the constant presence of sunshine over the Tagus River transforms this Portuguese capital into a mirror of a thousand colors, highlighting the city's unique architecture.

3. BUDAPEST, HUNGARY
The City of the Danube, Budapest is Hungary's capital and is filled with beautiful historic architecture, hot springs and sophisticated cuisine. It's hard not to be taken aback by all this city has to offer, earning its spot as one of the more vibrant cities in Europe and a definite mainstay for those looking to become completely absorbed and inspired.

4. LIMA, PERU
Lima has absolutely earned its spot as the capital of Peru. With a population close to 10 million people, anyone can find their place in this massive city. Lima may be known by the world for their food—they claim three restaurants in "The World's 50 best restaurants"—but the city has much more to offer than fine dining.

5. CAPE TOWN, SOUTH AFRICA
A bustling metropolis on the coast, Cape Town has unmatched views and a backdrop that can't be beat: It sits on a peninsula beneath Table Mountain. It's known as one of the most wanderlust-y cities for good reason. With plenty of diverse offerings such as unique flora and fauna, drool-worthy beach side towns, and a cool urban edge, this city is a must-visit cultural destination.

6. MEDELLÍN, COLOMBIA
There's lots to uncover in this Colombian city that's nicknamed the "City of Eternal Spring" and now best known for its textile manufacturing industry. It's pulsing with discos, street performers and a cultural renaissance that's put the city on the radar of many travelers who were once wary of the effects of its notorious cocaine cartel in the 1980s. With a population of 2.5 million people, each neighborhood feels like its own city, so there's plenty to explore.

7. BORDEAUX, FRANCE
The city of Bordeaux is one of France's most charming cities. Known as the "City of Art and History," it is home to some 360+ historical monuments, with some buildings dating back to Roman times.

8. KIEV, UKRAINE
The cultural capital of Ukraine, Kiev is full of golden domes and eclectic architecture which puts it on the map as the top stop to visit in Ukraine. Plus, it's got a lively underground arts and nightlife scene with a bohemian vibe that's really focused on boosting their own local performers and musicians to drive the scene.

9. VALENCIA, SPAIN
Compared to its vibrant older sisters Madrid and Barcelona, Valencia has a calm, cool, and collected vibe. It's a mixture of contemporary masterpieces and intricate architecture from the past—and the locals have a deep appreciation for their culture paired with an eye for modern design and innovation.

10. STOCKHOLM, SWEDEN
Stockholm exudes a cool, fashion-forward vibe amidst its cobblestoned streets and medieval architecture. Spread across 14 islands and 57 bridges, this city is filled with both eclectic and traditional neighborhoods, all colorful and cozy at the same time. Luckily it's easy to stroll around, so you never feel too disconnected from exploring the other parts.

By Mary Murphy, Marketing Coordinator, GlobeKick with Arielle Crane, Community Manager, AND CO.

Chapter 5

FINDING THE BEST LIVING SITUATION FOR YOU

By Matt Prior
⚑ Peak District, England

It's such an amazing time to be alive. The furthest corners of the globe are now easily within reach, and much more accessible for work and play. No longer do you need to splash the cash, exhaust your savings, and borrow heavily from loved ones to afford to live in a new land. What great news this is for us digital nomads!

ANYWHERE

At this stage, the employment ball is rolling and the puzzle pieces are falling into place. You've landed on your chosen host city (or at least narrowed down your list). You've got work in the pipeline, your laptop is fully updated and you're ready to hit the ground running. What's your next move?

The first thing to ask yourself is, "What do I want to be near?" Does the convenience of city life hold you in its fond, sympathetic clutches? Is there anything better than being within a stone's throw of a gorgeous white sandy beach? Can you imagine stepping out of your dwelling of choice and being surrounded by the most mindblowing landscapes?

> **"THE FIRST THING TO ASK YOURSELF IS, 'WHAT DO I WANT TO BE NEAR?'"**

As the age of the digital nomad is in full swing, the idea of working remotely via internet is a fast-growing lifestyle choice, and we as a collective group of people are adding to the demand of those willing to house us. Hospitality networks online have been given a new life with the number of digital nomads wanting to find their perfect home overseas. There is certainly one idea that has seen a rise in interest: the pioneering co-living space. It's the new go-to for many freelancers and digital nomads planning their lives elsewhere.

CHAPTER 5

WHAT ARE CO-LIVING SPACES?

Co-living spaces are a budding concept. Communities of freelancers have seen the exponential benefits of coming together and creating a co-living/co-working hub, saving money on living costs, working with like-minded, motivated freelancers and continuing to travel the world. This next evolution of the WeWork model has proliferated over the past five years.

Living and working alongside other freelancers and having an amazing social atmosphere within a comfortable environment may be just what you are looking for as you start your own nomadic lifestyle. It offers the complete digital nomad experience (i.e. living and working abroad) along with the safety net of having a relatable group of nomads around as you make the leap into a new lifestyle.

These co-living spaces can be determined based on your monthly budget. Indeed, there are a growing number of communities forming around the world, giving every opportunity for digital nomads to flourish with one another. From my own experience, the houses are modern, the people are super cool, and the location is exactly what is needed when staring at a laptop screen for many hours of the day.

ANYWHERE

The leaders of each community will have vetted the best places to live to determine the following:

- **Cost:** What is total cost of rent plus electricity and water bills?
- **Length of stay:** Is it cheaper to book longer term, or does the group want to move on after a certain amount of time?
- **Wi-Fi speed:** Can the connection strongly hold download/upload speeds for 10 to 20 laptops plus phones?
- **Local amenities:** Are there shops easily accessible for food, drink and other supplies?
- **Trust:** Has the owner provided security locks and lockers?
- **Living and sleeping space:** How many community members can the place hold (comfortably) at one time?
- **Transportation options:** Are there bicycles, scooters, cars that are available for use? If not, is the locale walking-friendly?
- **Surrounding area:** Are there opportunities for discovery and amusement to keep the group engaged?

As you can see, there is plenty to consider for each community, but this is a good checklist to also use for yourself, should you wish to plan and program your own co-living setup with friends, colleagues or other collaborators.

CHAPTER 5

WHERE CAN I FIND A CO-LIVING SPACE ABROAD?

There are a few ways to seek and nail down what you are looking for. If you have a location in mind, then you can search for co-living communities in that area. Each community will have a plan already drawn up in advance, so that new and existing members can join or re-join the clan as they move from gorgeous home to gorgeous home.

For instance, if the Mediterranean coast sounds like somewhere you want to be for an extended period, you will find that there is a community called **Sun and Co** (www.sun-and-co.com). If you want to move around, country-to-country, continent-to-continent, get in touch with the **Wi-Fi Tribe** (www.wifitribe.co). **Outsite** (www.outsite.co) is a third company, newly-formed, which programs co-living houses across the California coastline, Puerto Rico, and even Brooklyn. **Nomad House** (www.nomadhouse.io) is another option.

These are just three options within a mounting list of such, check out websites such as **CoWoLi** (www.cowoli.com/coliving) and **Nomad List** (www.nomadlist.io), which both rank and review hundreds of amazing places where you work, explore and enjoy the co-living dream.

NOMAD TIP:

"Once you have confirmed your interest in a place, make sure you set up a Skype meeting and have some questions prepared for the homeowner regarding safety and the surrounding area. That way, you project professionalism to the home owners, who will feel more relaxed by your enquiries into living at their house."

Matt Prior, Journalist
Peak District, England

CHAPTER 5

WHAT ABOUT A MORE PRIVATE-LIVING SPACE ABROAD?

Perhaps a curated, community-focused setup isn't for you. I've personally enjoyed traveling alone, or with a small group of people, and I've found value in the following resources.

Airbnb (www.airbnb.com) is an ever-growing app and website that allows you to live like a local someplace you've never been. Depending on availability, you can request to stay from one night to as many months as the local government or your visa allows. Costs significantly decrease in some cities based on your length of stay. Similar to a hotel, you can see all the amenities you have available during your stay.

A few tips here: First, make sure that the Wi-Fi is decent! Also, be sure to thoroughly read the reviews. If a location has very few reviews, proceed with caution. I recommend thoroughly vetting the neighborhood and surrounding areas before booking. Finally, more often than not, the adage "If it seems too good to be true, it probably is" applies. Do your homework, as it can be difficult to back out of these arrangements once they've been booked.

Couchsurfing (www.couchsurfing.com) is a free service that allows members of the nomad and travel community to "crash" at fellow members' homes for free during their travels. Once you sign up for the app, simply create a profile (be sure to let your personality shine!) and request to contact a host. Though the service is free, I recommend paying the verification fee to ensure hosts feel safe hosting you.

ANYWHERE

Couchsurfing is a resourceful app because you can choose who to stay with depending on sleeping arrangements (private room, couch, etc.), select residences with strong Wi-Fi, and vet hosts based on their ability to serve as a guide should you wish to explore the area. You might also offer to help your host with their social media presence or website, or barter your professional serves in other ways that make sense. If the host is a business-owner, offer to pitch in for an hour a night so that you can maximize your length of stay and save a ton of cash on monthly rental fees.

House-sitting: In my experience, house-sitting is the best and most cost-effective way to acquire accommodations while living and working as a nomad. There are some fabulous places available that need your tender loving care, and most often come equipped with a friendly pet of some kind.

To get involved with services like **Trusted House Sitters** (www.trustedhousesitters.com), you'd simply pay a small annual sign-up fee with the house-sitting website and set up an honest and approachable profile. After that, you'll be able to apply to the awaiting house owners. The stark contrast in homes will become apparent soon after (I once saw a castle on there!).

NOMAD TIP:

"Have a solid income stream that is in line with the cost of living in the desired destination(s). Having a backup plan in place in the case that income stream runs dry is also crucial."

Sara Graham, Communications Strategist
Turin, Italy

ANYWHERE

DETERMINING A FAIR RENTAL RATE

Renting apartments from the likes of Airbnb is a happy compromise for those who don't want to spend their money on hotel rooms for long periods, but want more privacy than what is available in a hostel. You can spread yourself out, literally and figuratively, and have more of a chance to cook for yourself, spend an hour in the shower, and most likely have a much better internet connection.

However, in terms of determining a fair rate, you must first research the local cost of living. For this, I recommend **Numbeo** (www.numbeo.com), a website that is constantly updated with the latest local prices of supermarkets, short/long-term rental costs, fuel and electricity costs, alcohol, and anything else you need to know. You can even compare two places to decide which one is more cost-effective. You can really get to know a country or city this way, and it will certainly help with forming a monthly budget. For example, a rental apartment in Bangkok can be much cheaper than a flat in a European city, but Bangkok's western food choices may be more expensive than in the actual west.

Another important consideration is the cost of transport. Again, using Bangkok as an example (I lived there long enough to know!), it is cheap to get anywhere in the city or indeed outside of it, whereas in Europe or America, the costs are much higher.

CHAPTER 5

THE BIG TAKEAWAY: DO YOUR HOMEWORK

If you find your accommodation through a private website, check Google for reviews. Fact-checking is vital if you want to know what you are getting for your money, especially since the first time you'll physically meet your new home and/or host will be upon your arrival. If you are using hospitality networks such as Airbnb, positive online reviews are the lifeblood of their business, so it is in their best interest not to oversell and under-deliver.

Before confirming a place, make sure you are aware of what the local neighborhood holds. Ask yourself these questions before booking:
- Do you have shops nearby?
- Is it on a busy street or quiet area?
- Are there regular, accessible transport links?
- Are there security guards?
- Is there a neighbor you can contact in an emergency?

Lastly, to clarify that you are happy with the safety of yourself and your belongings, be sure to check the latest goings-on via **My Local Crime** (www.mylocalcrime.com), the world's largest and most comprehensible map showing local crimes.

ABOUT THE AUTHOR

Matt Prior grew up in a small town in Herfordshire, England, but since then his nomad travels have taken him all around the world and he most recently spent four years living in Thailand and Southeast Asia. Says Matt, "All I need is my laptop, my DSLR and a decent cup of tea, and I am on ready to take on the world."

@thelonelytravellermatt

@thelonelytravellermatt

www.thelonelytraveller.co.uk

Chapter 6

THE ULTIMATE DIGITAL NOMAD PACKING LIST

By Jennifer Miller, Editor, Tortuga Backpacks
◊ Ontario, Canada

If you're toying with the idea of pursuing a nomadic lifestyle or contemplating a long-term trip, the way you pack will be significantly different than the way an average traveler would. No doubt you'll have special considerations that stationary workers and casual travelers don't have. So, what do you pack when you travel as a digital nomad?

These packing tips will help you be a productive and happy remote worker–from anywhere!

ANYWHERE

DIGITAL NOMAD BACKPACKS

Let's start with what you're putting everything in: your backpack. As a frequent—in fact, constant—traveler, you don't want to waste time rummaging around your bag, or waiting for one at luggage carousels. And, you want to make sure your stuff is safe.

When selecting a backpack, make sure you look for a product that:

- Provides numerous pockets for top-notch organization
- Has a TSA-friendly panel for your laptop
- Has zippers that let you lock up
- Is carry-on size
- Is built to last (you'll be taking it everywhere, after all)

One option to consider: Tortuga's Outbreaker backpack (available in two sizes: 35-liter and 45-liter). As a digital nomad, I love that I can easily slip my laptop in and out of the bag and it's protected in its own pouch. The built in organizational panels and zippered compartments that make it easy for me to find a charger, toothbrush, pair of socks, or whatever else
I may need quickly.

For the extreme Type A's among us, Tortuga also offers packing cubes for meticulous compartmentalization. The wet/dry bag is perfect for stashing dirty laundry, or perhaps that damp swimsuit or muddy pair of shoes. Add the packable duffle, which is conveniently exactly the dimensions of a personal item on major airlines as overflow space for those few things you're inevitably going to pick up along the way.

When it comes to which bag to choose for heading to the coffee shop or co-working space, a well-designed, waterproof daypack with well-padded shoulder straps is a must. Waterproof and durable are key if you're planning to carry laptop in it and you need it to hold up over the long haul as a digital nomad.

ELECTRONICS

Electronics (and the accessories that accompany them) are perhaps the biggest consideration and the most carefully selected items that remote workers will bring with them. Here's a good starting list:

- Laptop & case
- Mouse
- Kindle
- Smartphone
- Camera, extra batteries and case (optional if you have a smartphone)
- GoPro (highly optional)
- External battery
- Universal adapter, like the Loop all-in-one.
- Headphones
- Chargers
- External hard drive, or thumb drive (there are thumb drives with up to 1TB of space, of space, but most nomads opt for 32GB).
- A lock to keep it all safe in your bag or hostel locker

Before we move on, there are a couple more considerations for digital nomads and their electronics.

ANYWHERE

Laptop
I love my MacBook Air, but some digital nomads will want a computer that they can get repaired anywhere in the world (Apple doesn't have stores in a lot of the more popular destinations). For them, a netbook is a good option. Dell and HP are popular brands for this.

I've also tested out traveling with an Android tablet and keyboard combo. Though light, I found that I was a little slower working on it. So, it's fine for a month or two, but probably not a full year of travel.

Camera
Depending on the scope of your work, a smartphone camera might be good enough. For something with a higher photo quality, a mirrorless camera is the way to go. They're point-and-shoot size, but DSLR quality.

Electronics Insurance
Picking up some basic electronics insurance is likely a good idea. Think of insurance as investing in your future interests. As a nomad, you need to make sure you're protecting your stuff, and opting for an affordable yet comprehensive travel insurance policy is smart way to safeguard yourself against the cost of replacing valuable electronics.

Full disclosure: I've never purchased travel insurance. However, after sharing an office with the team at **WorldNomads** (a travel insurance provider) and getting an iPad swiped in Hawaii, I think that was a poor decision on my part, especially for those longer trips where I carried more electronics than usual.

If you're traveling with a lot of electronics, I recommend springing for insurance. With any policy, you'll need do your due diligence and read the fine print, since not all providers have your electronics

NOMAD TIP:
"Add extra money in your budget to fix and/or purchase new electronics. Computers get fried from constant motion, salt, sand, sun and charging in different voltages. Phones get dropped into squat toilets accidentally and break, SIM cards get lost, and all of this matters when being connected is your top priority."

Kelly Lewis, Founder, Go! Girl Guides
Nepal

covered in the base fee. Worth noting, "Claims for lost, stolen, or destroyed laptops and tablets fall under the travel insurance coverage for baggage," according to **Travel Insurance Review** (www.travelinsurancereview.net).

Digital Storage Solution

Leave the giant external hard drive at home and get a 64GB or 128GB USB drive or SD card ($20 to $100+ depending on make/model). These things are so small you barely even notice them in your computer and are incredibly valuable if your job requires you to work with large files.

Headphones

I use my headphones pretty much every day whether I am working, at the gym, or just wandering the city. You will want to invest in a good pair that can block out the noise while you're working at cafes or co-working spaces. If you are going to be taking regular client calls, spring for over-the-ear headphones with a dedicated microphone so you don't have to worry about noise in public areas.

Travel Speaker

If you work on a team like I do, it's nice to have music playing on a portable Bluetooth speaker that everyone can listen to. These are fairly inexpensive and easily fit in the side pocket of your backpack. Plus, they're instant party starters at hostels.

HDMI Cable

It may seem like a strange thing to carry, but my HDMI cable has actually saved me more times than I can count. Costing less than $10, they take up almost no room, and allow you to connect to TVs and external monitors; perfect for working or watching movies on a bigger screen.

Kindle (or other e-book reader)
Some people might disagree with me on this, but if you're like me, you spend a lot of time reading on flights, buses, and trains. A Kindle is much easier to read on than a phone, and you can store hundreds of books—like this one—to last your entire trip.

Clothing
Of course, you are also going to be living out of your bag, so you'll need more than just work gear. Doing laundry while traveling is much easier, and less expensive, than you might think.

For clothes, digital nomads—who are usually longer term travelers, as well—should still stick to the seven-day rule. I'll often allow myself a couple of extra pairs of underwear and one nicer outfit when I'm on the road for months at a time, since I want to feel like myself (even if I'm working outside of my comfort zone).

For clothes, here's a good place to start:
- 5 to 7 days' worth of shirts, socks, and underwear
- 1 warm jacket, for long flights and colder weather locations
- 1 pair of comfortable shoes: Unless you're planning some multi-day climbs, you don't need special shoes to travel.
- 1 pair of flip-flops
- 1 bathing suit
- 1 pair of zip-off pants: Far from the most "on trend" option, these are nice to have in places where the weather can change at any moment.
- 1 pair of dark jeans: Dark jeans are versatile enough to be worn around town or to nicer restaurants and meetings.
- 1 pair of shorts
- 1 pair of mesh shorts, for home & sleeping

ANYWHERE

I'll also make sure that I can work out in at least one of these outfit combos, usually basic colored leggings and a T-shirt I don't mind getting dirty, since staying healthy on the road is so important.

Professional Outfit

You never know what opportunities might arise while you are traveling, so it definitely makes sense to bring at least one nicer button down shirt. Dark jeans and sneakers will suit you fine for nicer settings, but if you are trying to make a good impression with a potential client or investor, your Tiger Beer tank top isn't going to cut it.

Toiletries

Traveling for months at a time with only a 3-oz. bottle of shampoo is rough. While I won't detail every item you'll need to pack, here are some essential items to include in your own list:

- A bar of soap, rather than body wash
- Collapsible bottles
- Lip balm, tweezers, nail clippers, & basic medications
- Travel-sized deodorants
- A comb, not a brush
- Toothbrush & toothpaste
- Feminine hygiene products for women
- Band-Aids, ibuprofen and other basic first aid items

For travel beauty, keep it simple and versatile. Bar soaps last longer and do double duty as laundry soap, collapsible bottles allow you to refill, travel sized deodorant lasts forever, and a comb is more compact than a brush. **Stowaway Cosmetics** (www.stowawaycosmetics.com) makes travel-sized beauty products designed to be used on the road without taking up excessive space. As an added bonus, the products are cruelty-free!

CHAPTER 6

LIFESTYLE

Bring the items that make you happy since even when you are thousands of miles from home, you're not on vacation. This is your life, and you'll want the things that make you *you*. A few "comforts of home" you might want to pack if you're traveling longer term include:

Portable/Personal Coffeemaker
Unless you're renting an apartment or staying at a major hotel, chances are you won't have a coffee maker on hand. As such, the Bodum French Press Thermos is a great product to have if you can fit it in your bag.

Tupperware & Sporks
Charlie On Travel (www.charlieontravel.com), a green travel blog, recommends traveling with Tupperware and sporks to reduce plastic waste and be more eco-friendly. Hey, you've gotta carry those yummy airplane snacks in something, right? Her sporks are from **Light My Fire** (www.lightmyfire.com) and come with a case to keep your bag clean.

Collapsible Water Bottle
Charlie and I both agree on this one: Bring a water bottle, but make sure it's collapsible. That way, it doesn't take up a ton of room in your backpack when it's not in use.

Running Shoes & Yoga Mat
I hate running, but I've got to admit, it really is the most portable exercise. Stay active, and put those shoes to use on the trail, too (because hiking boots are a pain anyway, am I right?) As for yoga, my favorite mat is the foldable **Gaiam** (www.gaiam.com) travel mat, which is ideal for on-the-road flow sessions.

ANYWHERE

OTHER ESSENTIALS

The following items didn't fit nicely in our other categories, but they're no less important for digital nomads on the road:

- Passport (take a photo of your passport and have a print backup)
- Travel towel (or sarong)
- Travel flashlight or headlamp
- Eye mask & earplugs
- Pen
- Small notebook
- A day-bag
- A laundry line or rope
- Duct tape (because it can fix almost anything)
- One piece of non-digital entertainment, like a book or pack of cards

FINAL ADVICE FOR PACKING

Limit your "just in case" items to the things that you know you absolutely won't be able to get on the road (which isn't much, really) or would be in a huge pickle without (like a luggage lock).

> ## "NOW THAT YOUR BAG IS READY TO GO, ARE YOU?"

At the same time, bring the things that make you, well, you. Whether it's a coffee maker or your running shoes, you'll want to adapt, not ditch, your stationary life for your nomadic one. By traveling with few belongings and being as flexible as possible, you will make the logistics of the experience easier. Now that your bag is ready to go, are you?

Chapter 7

THE DIGITAL NOMAD'S TOOL BELT

By Simon Ammann
♥ Berlin, Germany

As an independent worker, you'll often spend a bigger chunk of your time organizing than you will being productive. Good news: The path to conquer that issue is paved with an ever-increasing number of miraculous digital helpers, some of which aren't worth the hassle of implementation.

ANYWHERE

According to Google Ventures' John Zeratsky, fancy tools give us yet another way to stay busy while avoiding the work we do. Instead, digital nomads will want to keep the organizational layer as thin as possible to get your core business rolling. Before opting-in to yet another digital utility, ask yourself three questions:

- Which problem do I have to solve right now?
- Is this app the simplest and most efficient solution to this?
- Can the new utility replace any existing tools or processes so that I can delete them?

Digital helpers are ideal for efficiently getting the back-work out of the way—without getting in your way—but you will want to separate the contenders from the pretenders. So, what do you need? Here's a starting list of tools and utilities for digital nomads.

> "FANCY TOOLS GIVE US YET ANOTHER WAY TO STAY BUSY WHILE AVOIDING THE WORK WE MEAN TO DO"

Apple Notes has covered me since my first iPhone back in 2010. Pre-installed on my phone and laptop, it lets me add notes, to do's and meeting minutes with ease. It syncs like it should and even works when you have those sudden while-driving-the-Autobahn-inspiration-moments. Just use your voice: "Hey, Siri."

CHAPTER 7

One of my top tips is to include a few contextual words below your memo to make remembering and searching for it easier after the fact. You can even use some handy keyboard shortcuts to help make taking notes a breeze.

Try this on a Mac:

1. Quickly opens the Notes app.

2. Creates a new note.
3. Boom. Start writing notes within seconds of having that ingenious idea pop into your head.

Want to upgrade the note-taking experience? Opt for **Evernote**, which can sync across devices.

Independent workers succeed when their communication game is on point. **Slack** (www.slack.com) is the go-to-tool for asynchronous communications across teams. Slack rolled out voice and video messaging late 2016 and plans to integrate screen sharing as well.

Speaking of communication, English is not my mother tongue–although my work spans across international teams. To cross check my spelling and grammar, I use **Grammarly** (www.grammar.ly), which uses AI to copyedit text. Grammarly helps me avoid misunderstandings and allows me to be as clear and accurate in my communications as possible. I even used it to proof this chapter!

ANYWHERE

Now, let's talk about protecting your work. Cloud backups (**Google Drive, Dropbox,** etc.) are sweeping away the data-anxiety by taking care of versioning and the whole offsite-backup-hustle. Make sure your preferred service allows for selective synchronization to keep precious GBs of space on your laptop free and your data safe and sound in the cloud. One practice to keep in mind: Don't forget to tidy up your cloud archive from time to time, as folders can often become cluttered with old documents and files.

Automation is the Holy Grail of simplification. Saving time by automating tasks is the ultimate goal for a freelancer. Your time and efficiency are critical. There are a few tools that are paving the way (**IFTTT** and **Zapier** connect apps via self-created or pre-built workflows), but in my daily location-independent work, these services have not yet found their place.

As for project management, there are plenty of options to explore. Let's focus on business operations for the moment. Recently featured by the App Store, **AND CO** (www.and.co) offers a sleek time-tracking tool that can be used to auto-populate invoices, if you work by the hour. The app also comes with expense-tracking features that sync with your bank account, a customizable contract template for kicking off new engagements and a business porting tool that shows you the money in/money out of your freelance business at a given point in time. AND CO has released a series of updates (like multi-currency invoicing) over the past several months that make it the most nomad-friendly freelance utility app in the game.

Working anywhere means that you can get paid and receive money anywhere. Online banks have made progress over the past several years. Mobile banking, expense tracking, income graphs, and low international fees are becoming a standard. **N26** (www.n26.com) is my favorite solution to date, offering all of the above and a neat

CHAPTER 7

looking black credit card. (Who said this wasn't important?) Downer: Since they only offer accounts for customers living in Europe, they couldn't replace my broken credit card when I was in Japan. This is an EU-only solution, but fin-techs like N26 are shooting up like mushrooms.

So, what makes a great addition to the digital nomad's tool belt? For me, a good rule of thumb is to trust my gut feeling: Is this something I enjoy using? If so, the rational part of my brain kicks in to check if it:

…is resilient (unlikely to be shut down; available when you need it)
…gives you back more time than it consumes (AKA solves the problem)
…integrates with accounts, tools or apps you're already using
…replaces one or more other instruments

My best advice: Test and learn. Play around with new apps, but be prepared to streamline and make cuts as needed. Start with the basics here, and then enhance and optimize based on your own habits and lifestyle.

ABOUT THE AUTHOR

Building his first website in 2002 and ever since absorbed by our digital advancements, Simon (www.smnmmnn.com) uses the momentum of the connected everything and designs and builds digital products for start-ups and Fortune 100 companies. Co-founding the yearlong project fourweeksgood (www.instagram.com/fourweeksgood) in 2017, Simon lives and works in 12 of the world's most livable cities to team up with like-minded businesses.

 @smnmmnn

 @smnmmnn

 www.simonammann.de

Chapter 8
VISAS 101

Though technology and modern travel may make the world feel borderless, digital nomads do need to follow the appropriate steps when spending extended periods of time living and working abroad. As you explore your options as a remote worker, the notion of acquiring a visa might feel like a daunting and complex process.

Indeed, it will be one of the more complicated – and more important – boxes you check before you proverbially set sail. Because travel and transport regulations vary from country to country, this chapter has been written from the perspective of a U.S. citizen or permanent resident who aspires to live and work abroad. We'll begin with some background information on visas, and then dive into the types of visas you'll need to pursue should you continue on your path of becoming a digital nomad.

As a reminder, this chapter is designed as a 101 to the subject of

ANYWHERE

visas. We strongly recommend diving into more specific research depending on the regions you plan to visit and, ultimately, call home.

WHAT IS A VISA, ANYWAY?

A visa is an endorsed document that allows people to enter into other countries for a specified period of time. Visas exist to provide countries with a traceable record of who is in their country at a given time, and this data is used for anything from tourism planning to national security. Unlike passports, visas share similar conventions so the local authorities in a given country can understand its contents no matter where the traveler has originated from.

The information within a visa tells the country you're entering who you are, why you are there and for how long you plan to stay. Each country will have its own entry requirements for visitors, and they can vary based on an entrant's nationality. For this reason, it's important to thoroughly research the visa procedure for your unique circumstances prior to planning a move abroad.

WHAT KIND OF VISA DO NOMADS TYPICALLY USE?

There are two overarching visas that apply to any country: immigrant (in which you become a citizen of that country) and nonimmigrant (whereby you do not become a citizen of that country, and are there for temporary travel).

Then, there are four types of travel visas.
Type 1: Tourist Visa
Type 2: Immigration and Naturalization Visas (included by marriage)
Type 3: Student Visas (for studying abroad)
Type 4: Business/ Working Visas

CHAPTER 8

Most digital nomads visit and travel to other countries on a tourist visa. A tourist visa is a temporary stamp of approval that you are welcome in that country for the specified time period, for the specific intent of travel. Though you will be working while you are there, if your job is agnostic to the country, you'll most likely be able to get away with a tourist visa.

By nature, tourist visas are temporary and expire within a set time frame. For tourist visa holders entering the U.S., for example, that duration is six months. Tourist visas are one of the underlying forces compelling nomads to be, well, nomadic. You can visit and live in several different countries on tourist visas so long as you're packing up and moving along within the expiration deadline.

The specific terms of the visa are, of course, critical to fully understand before embarking on your journey. Some countries, like China, impose strict exit requirements, mandating that tourists exit the country (even with a long-term, multiple entry visa) every 30, 60 or 90 days.

Most countries do not mind if you do business online while visiting their country. After all, this isn't much different than a executive taking time out of her family vacation to take a call or catch up on emails. That said, if you are soliciting local business as a nomad, you might be required to apply for a work visa. Clearly, this is somewhat of a grey area. For example, if you are compensated to housesit while abroad, does that constitute soliciting business? How about if you take on a small client in the city you're visiting?

ANYWHERE

Take the time to research the laws of the specific countries you will be working in. Visit nomad forums and message boards and ask people who are either there currently or who have recently lived (and worked) there. Keep in mind that operating under a veil of ignorance could get you into trouble, which might result in your getting banned or blacklisted.

Want a quick gut-check on the countries you plan to visit? **VisaCentral** has an easy-to-use lookup tool (www.visacentral.com/visa-quick-check) to help kick off your research.

HOW CAN NOMADS OBTAIN A VISA?

Some countries will require its visitors to apply for a visa in advance. Other countries streamline the process and even allow you to easily renew a tourist visa should you choose to extend your stay. We recommend acquainting yourself with the general rigidness of a country's visa application process well in advance, so you can be prepared in the event of a long and drawn-out process.

Of important note: Some countries will not allow you to enter their country, or even apply for a visa, if your passport is on track to expire within the next six months. An initial step you should take in the process of becoming a nomad is to renew your passport, if needed.

U.S. → Abroad

If you are a U.S. citizen, some countries will not require you to apply for a visa up until a certain point. For example, if you are travelling anywhere Australia, a visa is required regardless if you are U.S citizen or not. However, if you are travelling to Canada, no visa is required for stays under 180 days. For specific information regarding the visa policy for the countries you wish to visit, head over to the U.S. Department of State's resource on Passports & International Travel.

CHAPTER 8

If you do end up needing a visa, a good place to start the process is at the embassy website for the nation you intend to visit. There, you can fill out a visa application form online. It can take anywhere from two weeks to two months to review the application, and at that point, if approved, the consulate will mail you a visa that attaches to your passport. You can expect to pay anywhere from $50 to $200 to complete the visa application process.

Abroad → U.S.
If you are a non-U.S. citizen and your nomadic travels take you stateside, you'll need to apply to and be approved by the U.S. Department of State. The visa requirements will differ based on your nationality. To complete the application online, visit the **Electronic System for Travel Authorization**, or ESTA (www.esta.cbp.dhs.gov/esta).

Currently, there are 38 countries participating in the **Visa Waiver Program** (VMP), which allows people from these select countries to visit the U.S. without a pre-authorized visa. If you're from one of these countries, like New Zealand, Switzerland or the UK, you're in luck! No visa is needed.

WHAT DO YOU DO IF YOUR VISA EXPIRES?
As you might imagine, the rules vary by country. For example, in the U.S. you must apply with USCIS before your authorized stay, denoted on your admission stamp or paper Form I-94, expires. It's recommended that you apply well in advance of your expiration date. The long lead times that applications can take bring up an important point. As a digital nomad you're no doubt used to living your life on the web. Instant banking, instant communications—everything is real time. However, when working with federal agencies, things tend to move slower. A *lot slower.* Always build lead time into your planning

87

ANYWHERE

for applications and renewals, because they can take weeks, if not months to go through.

WHEN DON'T YOU NEED A VISA?

If you're planning to live as a nomad within your own country, you obviously will not require any sort of visa. Just pack your bags and go. That said, some countries are making it easier than ever to go in between partner countries. VisaCentral's quick-check tool is a great place to look if you are unsure where to go and want to prioritize a country with lax visa policies. For U.S. residents, you'd be surprised by how easy it can be to go in and out of many countries. In fact, U.S. citizens get access to 174 countries in the world by way of having an up-to-date passport. Instead of applying in advance, you'll speak with a border agent who will process your visa upon your arrival.

Part of your responsibility as a digital nomad is navigating the laws of the countries you are departing and entering. Given the complexities of the global landscape, it's critical to do your due diligence and thoroughly research your visa obligations early in your planning process.

CHAPTER 8

Chapter 9

HOW TO FIND WORK AS A NOMAD

By Jessy Coulter
♡ Puntarenas, Costa Rica

As remote work opportunities expand, online job boards and resources have popped up to help nomads and aspiring remote workers find fulfilling short- and long-term gigs to sustain them while they're living and working abroad.

This chapter is designed to give you a quick rundown of resources and best practices that you can begin using right now to secure work opportunities as you plan for your nomadic life.

ANYWHERE

RELEVANT JOB BOARDS FOR FINDING REMOTE WORK

AND CO's Gig List (www.and.co/gig-list): You don't always need to do the hunting. AND CO offers a free weekly email that curates the top ten remote roles of the week across a variety of skills.

We Work Remotely (www.weworkremotely.com) offers a searchable database of remote positions across more than eight categories, from marketing to dev-ops and everything in between.

Jobspresso (www.jobspresso.co) lists remote positions across a range of categories and offers the option of creating a profile and posting your resume for employers to see.

Remote.co (www.remote.co) lists remote positions across 10+ categories. The job board is user-friendly and their blog offers tips and best practices for remote work.

Working Nomads (www.workingnomads.co) lists remote positions under 15 categories, including Legal and Finance. Set up a profile to keep tabs on bookmarked jobs, but beware that sometimes the listings can be out of date.

Remotely Awesome Jobs (http://remotelyawesomejobs.com) offers a list of remote opportunities tailored for technical and programming professionals. An additional resource curated for this crowd is **Authentic Jobs** (www.authenticjobs.com).

Outsourcely (www.outsourcely.com) is the LinkedIn of the remote job market. The platform will ask you to set up a profile and have at least one of your past job positions verified in order to be able to start applying for positions on their site. Here, you can chat with employers, see how many others have applied for the position, and participate in a referral bonus program.

Dribbble (www.dribbble.com) is a site that allows UX/UI designers to share their work and see what others are working on. Dribbble's job board is great as it allows you to easily search by Remote roles only. **Behance** (www.behance.net/joblist) is another designer resource with a robust jobs board.

AngelList (www.angel.co) is a job board specific to startups, many of which are hiring for contract and/or "Remote OK" professionals. To begin, set up a profile that includes your employment background. Once you've done that, you can apply to jobs with a single click and message employers. Filter by "Remote OK" in the job search to limit your outreach to only those companies open to partnering with nomads like yourself.

The Muse (www.themuse.com) offers a job platform with opportunities filtered by position, job level and company size. As an added benefit, The Muse offers top notch information including career coaching/advice and company profiles.

Glassdoor (www.glassdoor.com) allows you to search jobs through a keyword search, as well as setting up a profile with your resume. To start, they will ask you to submit one review of a company you have worked at or with, and this can be anonymous.

ANYWHERE

Indeed (www.indeed.com) is a job aggregator that allows you to search jobs by keyword and location. Since most jobs here are full-time and on-site, you will need to use keywords like "remote," "freelance" or "contract" to identify the right opportunities.

LinkedIn (www.linkedin.com) is an obvious place to search, and makes it very easy to apply for opportunities. Similar to Indeed, since this network is more targeted to traditional opportunities, you'll need to use keywords in your search to find remote-friendly opportunities.

NOMAD TIP:

"If you're on Slack already (which is increasingly common), consider joining communities there to stay connected with the broader nomad community. NomadList's Slack Channel, for example, brings together 7,000+ nomads from around the world. You can join at www.join.nomadlist.com."

Sofia Miller, Independent Designer
Porto, Portugal

ANYWHERE

GENERAL BEST PRACTICES FOR THE REMOTE JOB SEARCH

Here are some words to the wise as you job hunt as a nomad:

- **Be sure to keep your profiles complete and up-to-date.** This is especially important when it comes to applying to opportunities via established networks like LinkedIn, AngelList and Indeed.

- **Maintain a spreadsheet of ideal companies or opportunities you come across in your search.** Mark the status of your application, so you don't have to rely on your memory when it comes time to follow-up.

- **Do your homework!** Without the ability to visit an office or meet the team in person, use resources like Glassdoor and The Muse to get a sense of salary expectations (helpful for calculating your rate), cultural watch-outs and other red flags.

- **If you can, apply via the network or job board, but also use LinkedIn to identify the hiring manager and reach out directly.** Tools like **Email Checker** (www.email-checker.net) allow you to verify someone's email address without ever hitting send.

- **Although you might be traveling in a faraway land, take proactive steps to remain "on the radar" in key markets.** This might be as simple as participating in a Twitter chat or Slack channel, contributing thought leadership via LinkedIn Pulse or Medium, offering to participate in a webinar, or connecting with recruiters who pair opportunities in your industry. Make an effort to keep your personal brand relevant and fresh in the markets that will hire you.

- **Most remote workers can benefit by setting up a simple online portfolio that quickly establishes their skills, previous work/ partners and contact information.** Tools like **Squarespace** make this relatively easy, but if you want to go even more minimalistic, check out **about.me**, which reduces the friction of buying and maintaining a formal domain.

All of this information is just the start in beginning your search for remote work. Once you've found the best places to surface opportunities within your industry, schedule a block of time each month (or perhaps once every two weeks) to browse job boards and contact employers. If you're mostly working on projects, scanning and applying for roles will likely become a core part of your new business strategy and a requirement for keeping your pipeline flowing as a remote worker.

ABOUT THE AUTHOR

Jessy Coulter is a contributor for Hustle&Co, the leading publication devoted to educating and empowering the future workforce. A born and raised California girl, she is now living in beautiful Costa Rica. She is a self-taught remote hustler, recent graduate from CSU Chico, and avid traveler. Jessy loves the digital nomad life, and is constantly networking in order to find new opportunities and new people to meet. When not working, she loves watching movies or planning her next trip.

 @jessycoulter
 @jessycoulter

Chapter 10

EFFECTIVE COMMUNICATIONS STRATEGIES FOR NOMADS

By Rena O'Brien
Toronto, Canada

Due to the general lack of face-to-face interactions with clients, colleagues and collaborators, digital nomads face unique challenges when it comes to communication. This chapter will explore best practices for articulating the details of your projects, and your overall value, while you live and work remotely.

ANYWHERE

MANAGING EXPECTATIONS

Perhaps this is your first remote gig, or maybe it's your fifth. Regardless, let's say you're fresh and ready to start the first day of work, eagerly sitting at your computer at 8 a.m., waiting for the first tasks to come across your desk. When 9 a.m. rolls around and you haven't heard a word, what do you do? Do you send an email? Should you call the hiring manager? These types of lapses in communication can become all too common for digital nomads if you fail to manage expectations from the very first interaction with your employer.

From early conversations, you should ask relevant questions about your assigned role as well as what the team and what your direct manager will expect of you. These early talks will help both sides gauge productivity patterns from the get-go and will demonstrate that you're proactive enough to take on a remote position.

Now you're set up, you've asked all the key points to your role and you're ready to move forward. It doesn't stop there. The key things to remember about expectations is that managing them also means sometimes pushing back. Just because you're working from a remote location, doesn't mean a client is justified in emailing you at 11 p.m. with last minute changes, or maybe it does. Expectations can either be missed, met, or exceeded. It's up to you to clearly communicate them and come to a mutual agreement with your clients or colleagues.

VIDEO CHAT IS YOUR FRIEND

A number of video services are at your disposal these days, and the majority of them are free. Whether you're using **Google Hangouts, Slack, Zoom** or something else, these services exist to help people communicate more efficiently and with a bit more warmth than an email or chat messaging program would.

NOMAD TIP:
"Relentlessly stick to your brand image! This principle is indispensable for growth because it will guide all of your business decisions, help keep your venture lean and ensure that your customers or clients understand what you're offering."

Peter Lovisek, CEO, Fossil Realm, Inc.
Ottawa, Canada

NOMAD TIP:

"Life as a digital nomad does not mean that you are always on vacation. You may be beachside in Colombia with a cocktail at your 'desk', but you still have work to do. If you want to be successful, you need to put in your hours and be as proactive as possible."

Elijah Masek-Kelly
La Paz, Bolivia

If you can't communicate a task, update, or thought in less than a couple of sentences, consider moving to video. Going back and forth trying to come to a solution results in wasted time on both ends and can leave both parties frustrated.

Test and use your video chat as often as possible, making sure that internet connections are secure and reliable. This ensures that you can hop on if needed and that you're not spending endless time fiddling with your mic or video. If you're in a coworking space, keep your headphones handy and take out some quiet spaces to avoid distracting background noise

SLACK HACKS & OTHER TOOLS

The advent of Slack ushered in a new era of team communications. My current Slack account has hundreds of channels available, and I use the tool in a variety of ways. Slack is great for one-off questions across teams, and for keeping in touch with updates from other teams. It's also a great culture-building tool: I've had conversations about traveling with co-workers in Brazil, talked about the shows we're watching with colleagues on the East Coast of the U.S. and formed game-plans with my counterpart, all via Slack (with emojis and GIFs, to boot).

Slack is free for small teams; however, if you're working with a bigger company you (or more likely your employer) will pay a premium for multiple users. **Zapier** has written about some of the best project management software apps currently out there, with a handy comparison tool so you can make sure you're finding the best fit for your team. Head over to Zapier.com to learn more.

ANYWHERE

KEEP IT PROFESSIONAL

Living in Bali? Working from Denver for a team in Boston? No matter where you are, make sure you're set up to succeed in your role. This means having proper attire if you need to video chat with anyone, having reliable internet, and making sure your tech is updated with backups should you need them.

The perk of traveling is high on the list for a lot of digital nomads, but don't let that lull you into a false sense of vacation mode. This means clearly setting expectations and communicating your travel time, working out time zone issues, (use a calendar that adjusts for different time zones) and respecting other nomads. This not only has an impact on you, but can also have an impact on your company.

Co-working spaces exist for—you guessed it—working. Meeting new people is a leading benefit of nomadism, but this doesn't mean your desk mate wants to hear about all the countries you've traveled to (or plan to) as they are rapidly approaching a critical project milestone. Reserve small-talk for coffee breaks and meals, or better yet, ask your co-working buddy to join you at a local meetup or event.

The opposite side of the spectrum regarding human interaction is the solitude that can accompany a nomadic lifestyle. If you don't have a team that you communicate with daily, being alone in a new city can be daunting. Get out of your comfort zone and explore the city, sit at the bar in restaurants and ask the locals for their favorite spots. Go to meetups and hit up the forums for other nomads that are in your area. This is a great opportunity to meet some new friends, as well as potential future business contacts (keep this in mind as you consider ordering that third mojito).

CHAPTER 10

WORKING FROM A DIFFERENT TIME ZONE

Setting expectations at the beginning of a partnership will save you a lot of headaches when it comes to resolving potential time zone challenges with your client. If you're 12 hours ahead and expected to be on multiple video chats a day, you might find it hard to make this type of relationship work.

In many cases, however, nomads find ways to make it work and their employers are flexible when it comes to the time zone discrepancies. Fortunately, there are a number of tools available to keep the time zones straight, starting with **Google Calendar**. Other simple tools include **World Time Buddy** (worldtimebuddy.com) and **Calendy** (calendy.com), which syncs with Google Calendar to allow you to set and share your "available" hours with clients and collaborators. Once you're booked for a window, your schedule is blocked and you cannot double-book.

There are several characteristics that will make you an effective nomad, such as an open and positive demeanor and flexible approach to work. In addition to these, strong communication skills are imperative for nomads functioning within teams based in different regions and/or time zones. Manage expectations and over-communicate as a rule to keep projects on track and your clients up-to-date.

ABOUT THE AUTHOR

Rena O'Brien is a digital nomad spending the next few months traveling through Europe. She works in the tech industry and teaches yoga (in addition to a few other side gigs) in her spare time.

 @renaobrien, @havelovewill.travel

Chapter 11

SETTING YOUR BUSINESS GOALS

As you set sail on your new adventures as a nomad, you might feel liberated by your newfound freedom. Perhaps you are a full 12 hours ahead of your clients, working during their off-hours with minimal interruption. Or, maybe you've scheduled your projects in waves of sprints, balancing two weeks for intense work with two weeks of vacation each month. Regardless of the structure (or lack thereof) you've established in your new life, it's critically important to keep your career and your career goals on track.

Traditional corporate settings usually reinforce the idea of goal-setting via annual performance review cycles and regular check-ins with a manager. But how are you supposed to ensure you're growing and improving as a professional when you're a team of one? As is the case with many aspects of your life as a freelancer, the buck ultimately stops with you. This chapter is designed to provide a framework for goal-setting that help you move along your chosen career path as you trek around the world.

DETERMINE YOUR NORTH STAR

If you've opted to pursue a nomadic lifestyle, chances are you're the type of person who knows what they want out of life. You likely value work/life balance, personal health and happiness, and quality of life above things like financial gains and title increases. Knowing your own values is important as you approach goal-setting in your career because it helps you set parameters for your work life relative to your personal ambitions.

The first step to goal-setting as a freelancer is to shift your mindset to think of yourself as a business of one. As the founder, CEO and CFO of your own business, it's only natural that you need a create a business plan. What does your business stand for, and what are you setting out to do? These questions will ultimately help you determine your North Star.

Think about what it is you want your business to accomplish in its simplest terms. Some examples:
- "I want to help startups differentiate themselves through breakthrough AI."
- "My mission is to help brands be more relevant with their audiences by creating content that offers tangible value."
- "I want to build things that fundamentally change the way people view Industry X."

> **"SET A NORTH STAR. THINK ABOUT WHAT IT IS YOU WANT YOUR BUSINESS TO ACCOMPLISH IN ITS SIMPLEST TERMS."**

CHAPTER 11

Each of these statements is broad enough to apply to multiple clients and projects—95 percent of freelancers juggle two or more at a time, per an AND CO study—but limited enough to help you vet opportunities along the way. As you proceed in your career, think about how the partners and projects you take on get you closer to that North Star.

SET YOUR STANDARDS SKY-HIGH

Thinking about potential work opportunities in the context of your journey to your personal North Star will help you separate the things that will pay the bills and fulfill you from those that you simply take on to shore up some cash until your next trip. In addition to vetting based on your North Star, you might also find it helpful to create a simple scoring system for vetting partners and opportunities.

For example.
- **People**: Do you respect the potential partners? Are they ethical and trustworthy? Will you enjoy working with them?
- **Product**: Do you believe in the product or company overall? Are they building something that inspires you, or are they hawking something you don't exactly believe in? Are you inspired by what they're building?
- **Project**: What are the associated tasks of the opportunity? Will they push you or bore you? Keep in mind that a little pain can mean growth, and just because you're an independent worker doesn't mean it's best to take the easy route.

Gut check opportunities that come your way as a nomad with these simple criteria. You'll be surprised at how it changes the way you view potential clients and projects.

NOMAD TIP:

"If you don't have an accountant already, begin your search by asking your friends or fellow independent workers for a recommendation. Chances are, someone will have a great resource they can recommend, and you'll save the time researching to make sure the accountant is competent and reliable. You can also search reviews on Yelp and browse the website for the American Association of Certified Public Accountants (aicpa.org)."

Katie Perry, Editor, AND CO
Brooklyn, NY

CHAPTER 11

BE A PROACTIVE GOAL-SETTER

Anyone who has traveled will relate to the speed at which time passes when you're away from home. As a digital nomad, you might wake up one day and wonder where the past six weeks have gone. Setting monthly, quarterly and yearly goals will help you hold yourself accountable.

Goal-setting can be as simple as creating a running Google Doc or Asana project to keep you on task. The first step is the most important of all: write them down! For each goal, be sure to indicate how you plan to measure success. For example:

Bad goal: "I want to get more clients."
Good goal: "I want to double my number of recurring clients by Date X."

Bad goal: "I want to make more money."
Good goal: "I want to increase monthly revenue by 30 percent by expanding business offerings into social media and content."

Bad goal: "I want to get more local business."
Good goal: "Work on Spanish fluency and begin networking with local business owners to vet future opportunities. Set up three coffee meetings by Date X."

> **"A LITTLE PAIN CAN MEAN GROWTH, AND JUST BECAUSE YOU'RE AN INDEPENDENT WORKER DOESN'T MEAN IT'S BEST TO TAKE THE EASY ROUTE."**

ANYWHERE

After you've established detailed goals, make sure they are attainable by listing out strategies for accomplishing them. If you are scratching your head and coming up empty, you might need to revise the goal or make it a longer term initiative.

The final step is holding yourself accountable. Set recurring calendar invites to check in on your goals, and don't be afraid to adjust them along the way. Reward yourself when you reach a goal, and then set a new one to keep on striving.

CHAPTER 11

Chapter 12

TAX & LEGAL WATCH-OUTS FOR DIGITAL NOMADS

By Remi Alli
◉ Kentucky, USA

There are many legal risks that digital nomads should watch out for before taking the leap. Here are some insights into the legal and tax-related watch-outs you should be cognizant of as you begin your new life as a nomad.

Please note: This chapter is designed to provide some initial best practices to consider; however, it should not be substituted for the guidance of a registered tax accountant (we recommend that all digital nomads work with one) or legal professional, should you end up needing one.

ANYWHERE

PROACTIVELY REDUCE YOUR LIABILITIES
When working as a nomad, you'll need to do your due diligence to reduce any and all liabilities. This includes having copies of written company consent regarding your plans to work remotely from several locations. Equally important is maintaining backups of your work efforts, software, systems (like computer drives), and more to cover yourself in the event of unforeseen circumstances.

RESEARCH LOCAL & REGIONAL LAWS BEFORE YOU LEAVE
Many law libraries have terminals set up where non-attorney persons can access legal search engines (think Google for Law) for information on various legal-related information that is not easily accessible elsewhere. These include **WestLaw** (www.westlaw.com) and **LexisNexis** (www.lexisnexis.com) and anyone can use them without having an actual subscription, although you may have to pay per hour for this service.

When you track down a law library, ask the librarian where their patron access is located. If you find yourself having trouble navigating these resources, you can utilize the sites' reference attorneys (likely free of charge) via your phone or the online chat area on their site for help with this new material. Some law librarians can also help you with researching the local laws and legal structures of the countries of your choices. Tip: Ask for the "International Business" section on these sites.

ALWAYS BE TRANSPARENT ABOUT YOUR WHEREABOUTS
Be transparent regarding your whereabouts each time you relocate. Your company's IT team will often be able to tell if and when you are logging in from another country as your IP number will be different. Anything that goes through a company's network can and will be tracked. Ensure the terms of your remote engagement are clearly

communicated and that your manager and/or colleagues are up to speed on your location and availability.

BE DILIGENT ABOUT PAYING YOUR TAXES

IRS tax deductions are also something to consider. For U.S. tax purposes, depending on your citizenship, you could be classified as self-employed or as an independent contractor and your income earned as a nomad may be fully taxable.

Stating the obvious, just because you're not on U.S. soil does not mean you're off the hook when it comes to your responsibility to pay U.S. taxes. Stay on top of your reporting and payment schedule to simplify your work and personal life abroad. Need help? Seek the counsel of a registered accountant to help you prep and file taxes and navigate your new status. The additional expense will be well-worth the peace of mind, and it can even be written off as a business expense.

REGARDING RESIDENT STATUS

Foreign income exclusions might apply if you are a foreigner living and working abroad in the United States. This will depend on the tax laws of your citizenship abroad. You may not have to pay tax for your home country after taking advantage of exemptions; however, you may want to contribute to your country's social security system. The U.S. has a social security treaty with certain countries, meaning that social security payments made in the U.S. can sometimes be credited back to your home country.

NOTE: U.S. TAX LAWS APPLY TO U.S. "PERSONS"

U.S. "persons" generally include citizens, green card carriers, and resident aliens. The U.S. tax laws apply to work physically done in the U.S. or its territories. A U.S. firm can pay a citizen of another country to work overseas, but a 1099-Misc, W-2, or 1042-S will not be issued,

ANYWHERE

as none of these apply. A citizen of another country doing such work likely should also not fill out a W-9 or a W-8BEN. If a U.S. firm asks for either, it may indicate that they do not understand the reporting requirements and will erroneously issue forms that imply there is U.S. work involved. IRS publication 515. Thus, it is most important to ask your company for the specific documents that apply for your location and citizenship.

PAYING TAXES OUT OF STATE & OUT OF COUNTRY
Often, U.S. persons will pay taxes in the state they work, and not necessarily where their employer is based. For example, if your company is in Louisiana, but you work in Michigan, you'll pay Michigan taxes. Your employer likely should withhold taxes from your check for these state taxes if your home is considered your base office.

As a U.S. citizen, you'll file a U.S. tax return on all worldwide income. You would also get credit for foreign tax paid. If you are self-employed, your income is reported on Schedule C and you'll be required to file a tax return if your income from self-employment is $400 or more. You may not necessarily owe income tax, but you will likely owe around 15 percent of your net profit as self-employment tax (this amount will be applied to programs like Social Security and Medicare.

Even if you have a deduction, as an employee you'll likely only be entitled to any benefit if you itemize, and only for amounts over 2 percent of your annual gross income (AGI).

TAX DEDUCTIONS AS A NOMAD
- **Exclusive business deductions:** If you have a designated (separate) phone line and internet connection for business use, these costs are likely deductible. Long-distance phone

calls would also qualify here, although tax savings are modest as they are subject to a 2 percent AGI floor.
- **Housing deductions:** If your company requires you to maintain a home office, you might be able to write off part of your housing expenses as a result (this figure is calculated as the percentage cost of your home office relative to the entire home).
- **Cell phone and internet deductions:** If you have a business-designated phone or internet service, you can deduct that expense when filing your taxes. However, if your internet and phone services are a mix of business and personal, as many of ours are, then you will only be able to deduct long-distance calls or internet usage associated with your line of work.
- **Business-related travel costs:** Travel costs relevant to business trips and meetings can be written off. Personal travel expenses are fully taxable.

TROUBLE GETTING PAID?

According to the Freelancers Union, 71 percent of independent workers have had trouble getting paid by a client. Chances are, you've been stiffed before, and if you think it was hard getting invoices paid in your home country, just wait until you are thousands of miles away.

Since many unresolved payments result from miscommunications that stem from a shoddy or incomplete statement of work and freelance agreement, it's imperative for digital nomads to clearly articulate the terms of work and expectations upfront. Never begin work without a signed and secure contract in-hand. Need help getting started? Check out AND CO's free **customizable contract template** (www.and.co/freelance-contract).

ANYWHERE

If you're efforts to collect money due on an unpaid invoice are proving fruitless, you might consider sending a demand letter, before enlisting formal legal help. Enter AND CO's easy to use demand letter generator, **Williams&Harricks** (www.and.co/williams-harricks). For $3, AND CO will send a physical letter to the company, and will even even provide easy payment options to help you recoup your hard-earned dough.

Remember, most issues really depend on the laws of your location, so make sure to research and ask many questions with your personal advisor and company. Stay not only safe, but legal, as you live and work as a digital nomad.

ABOUT THE AUTHOR

Remi Alli has worked for publications such as Forbes and Investopedia, and in her work with Brāv, the premier online platform to manage conflicts (www.brav.org), has been featured in such journals including MONEY, TIME, The Huffington Post and Yahoo! She is an award-winning techie and three-time award-winning writer, with her most recent: a national legal award.

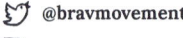 @bravmovement

www.brav.org

CHAPTER 12

Chapter 13

STARTING A NOMAD FAMILY? START HERE

By Amanda Napitu
♡ Bali, Indonesia

At some point in your life as a digital nomad the time may come for you to think about starting a family. Whether you and your partner set out on your nomadic journey together or you've met someone along the way, you now have a big decision to make: Do you continue with your nomadic lifestyle as you start a family, or do you return to your home country (one of them, at least) to a life of "normalcy?" From this point forward you're not just making decisions for yourself. You have to think about what's best for your growing family. It's a big responsibility.

I've been living in Indonesia for six years and have a daughter who is almost two years old. Here is my take on the highs and lows of being a parent away from your home country, and how to juggle parenting with remote work.

ANYWHERE

FAMILY SUPPORT

If you choose to raise a child in a foreign country, you'll most likely be doing it without the hands-on support of your extended family. Facebook and Skype are great for keeping in touch, of course, but they are no substitute for having someone there to look after the baby while you're on a big project or need to run a few errands. And by living far from your parents or in-laws, you're also forfeiting the benefit of cost-effective and trustworthy childcare.

There have been moments when I wished my family was closer, but since this is the only style of parenting I've ever known, I just get on with it. If you've been traveling for awhile, you're probably used to adapting to new situations, anyway. Facebook does come into its own when it comes to connecting with other parents in your area. It's great to be able to meet up with nearby nomads to socialize, share stories, and offer support.

BALANCING WORK TIME VS. FAMILY TIME

One thing that attracts many to the freelance lifestyle is the flexibility it provides—particularly when you're on the move. You can surf in the morning, enjoy a few beers in the afternoon, jump on a plane to somewhere new in the evening, and still have a sustainable income. This freedom and flexibility can be a mixed blessing as a parent. With no fixed schedule, it's easy to feel like you're getting the balance wrong, either by neglecting your children, your work, or yourself.

In the earliest sleep-deprived days especially, tensions can run high as you and your partner figure out how to distribute rest time, baby time, and work time. If you're both full-time freelancers, at least one of you will need to cut down your hours for a while. Make sure you discuss in advance about who that will be, and what your expectations are of each other as parents. If your work requires you to be online during certain scheduled windows, you'll also have to coordinate this with your partner. Babies sleep when they feel like it, not when you need them to.

FAMILY HEALTHCARE

One of the things you care about most as a parent is your child's health. As a single nomad you may have laughed in the face of health or travel insurance, but that level of irresponsibility won't cut it as a parent. Giving birth abroad is one thing that worries many mothers-to-be. For me, it seemed like the obvious choice since I'd made Indonesia my home and didn't want to be away for four to six months.

Why so long? Well, it's not a case of just jumping on a plane, popping the baby out, and flying back again. First, airlines won't let you fly after a certain point in your pregnancy. The limit can be anywhere from 28 to 36 weeks, so check your airline's policies before you book anything. Secondly, once the baby is born you'll need to get him/her a passport, maybe two, and a visa for the country you're returning to if required. Since obtaining a passport can take weeks or months, you can't count on being able to leave by a particular date.

I know plenty of mothers who opt to move back home for several months so they can benefit from a familiar health care system and have their family close by. I also know many people who have stayed in Indonesia to give birth and have had no problem at all. Everyone has different needs and priorities, so you'll need to work out what's right for you.

CHILDCARE AND EDUCATION

Perhaps second to your child's health is their education. You might not worry about it straight away, but it's something you'll have to figure out as they approach school age. Education options include local schools, international schools, homeschooling, and unschooling. Which one you choose will depend on how settled you are, how much you can afford for school fees, how much time you have, and what your views are on education.

If you don't like the idea of waiting four or five years before getting back to "normal" work, you'll need to think about either hiring a nanny or finding a daycare center. For me, having a nanny—although affordable—was just too distracting. Shut away in my home office I could still hear what was going on and I was often interrupted. Instead, we found a local daycare center (which is way more affordable and flexible than the nurseries marketed at expats) and my daughter has settled in really well.

EXPERIENCES AND PERSPECTIVE

It's easy to overlook the fact that letting your child grow up experiencing different cultures and countries is a great gift. It's more than just fancy summer holidays; they're living and adapting to different ways of life and learning what it means to be a citizen of the world. This is something that no expensive education can buy.

The same goes for you as a parent. As a nomad, you're not limiting yourself to one culture's perception of how to parent. Even if you don't agree with everything you experience in other countries, you will likely encounter new ways of doing things that just make sense. Having this broader perspective empowers you to make more conscious choices about your parenting, leading to better choices for your child. And isn't that what being a parent is all about?

CHAPTER 13

ABOUT THE AUTHOR

Amanda Napitu has journeyed from the UK to Indonesia through over 20 countries, freelancing as a writer and proofreader along the way. She is based in Indonesia with her husband and daughter for now, but still travels regularly. She writes for stuffwithwords.com and you can follow her adventures as a mum away from "home" at www.indomumma.com.

 www.facebook.com/Stuff-With-Words-153109521867022

 www.facebook.com/indomumma

 www.indomumma.com

Chapter 14

WELLNESS & SELF-CARE AS A NOMAD

By Aliya Rosenbloom,
Director of International Programs, GlobeKick
⚲ Cuba

Words like "wellness" and "self-care" have become buzzwords over the past several years. Submit a Google query on these terms and you'll be served with a staggering 550 million results. What exactly does self-care entail, and how can you work on living a healthier and more balanced lifestyle when you are living out of a suitcase or working in a foreign city?

ANYWHERE

Wellness is a tricky word and one that tends to indicate an arrival at a destination rather than the embracing of a journey. I like to think of wellness as the "personal happiness recipe." The recipe is different for every one of us and it can even change (and most certainly will) throughout our lives. Put another way, wellness is the pursuit of figuring out what we are personally made of and what makes our unique soul feel fullest, happiest and healthiest.

For me, wellness is about finding the perfect amount of all the necessary elements that make me who I truly am: What type of exercise makes me feel challenged, empowered, invigorated and centered? What foods make me feel nourished, sharp, full, and fueled? How much do I need to be around other people to feel socially supported, communally inspired, and externally motivated? How much time do I need to not be around others to feel the quiet of my mind and the power of recharging alone? How does my spirit feel most alive?

> "WELLNESS IS THE PURSUIT OF FIGURING OUT WHAT WE ARE PERSONALLY MADE OF AND WHAT MAKES OUR UNIQUE SOUL FEEL FULLEST, HAPPIEST AND HEALTHIEST."

Wellness and the personal happiness recipe is so much less about doing something in particular (or not doing something!) and so much more about learning who YOU are and what makes you operate at the fullest, brightest, best version of you. This is where the nomad part comes in. For many nomads, living a nomadic lifestyle is, in fact, a part of their own wellness journey.

NOMAD TIP:

"Spread the travel out. Spend at least one month in each location so your body can adjust. Maintaining a healthy lifestyle is key so probiotics and a regular fitness routine are essential for a healthy gut as lots of travel can wreak havoc on it."

Monika Pietrowski, Wellness Blogger
Chicago, IL

ANYWHERE

Traveling removes you from the familiar and throws you into an entirely new routine and an environment. This can impact your wellness journey by snapping you out of routines (say goodbye to your spin classes) or causing stress. A nomad lifestyle is ever-changing, and it requires you to explore the truest, unwavering parts of yourself that will be consistent no matter where you are in the world.

How will you cope while living in a city that doesn't have your favorite things? I've learned that I can lay out a yoga mat in any park in the world and come home to myself. I've found that journaling helps me remember and process my days as a nomad.

Overall, wellness is just an exploration and study of your own human nature. So the big question to consider is this: What makes YOU feel best? Answering this will unlock your own personal wellness story. No matter what others say wellness is or what the millions of fitness Instagram handles expose, it's about turning inward and getting curious about you.

Wellness isn't about limiting yourself from life's indulgences; rather, it's about working towards a sweet spot in between the polarities of life—the breakfast tacos to the green smoothies—and then being able to love yourself when you inevitably fall short of finding that harmony. Enjoy it all, be fully human and come home to yourself (whatever that means for you) when you need to. And you can do that anywhere in the world, at any time.

CHAPTER 14

ABOUT THE AUTHOR

Aliya is passionate about helping people step (or stretch!) out of their comfort zones and providing experiences for them where they are able to see what they are made of. With a Masters in Social Work and Community Development, Aliya has spent the past four years teaching yoga and providing experiences that unite teenagers and adults from over 35 countries together. Through yoga, traveling, and working with global populations, it is obvious to her that behind the millions of colors, races, and faces, we all inhale and exhale the same.

 @globekick

 @globekick

 www.globekick.com

Chapter 15

HOW TO BE A STUDENT OF THE WORLD

By Emily K. Olson
📍 Mexico

Being a digital nomad allows us to not only define the logistics of our preferred work—the when and where—but it also gifts us the opportunity to immerse ourselves in new cultures. At times the nomadic lifestyle can seem to be motivated solely by Wi-Fi strength; however, when we look around and unplug, a whole new experience awaits. This chapter will help you make the most of the cultural side of life as a nomad.

ANYWHERE

WHAT TO KNOW BEFORE YOU GO

To be a responsible traveler, and perhaps an unadmitted ambassador, it's important to learn a little bit about the places you plan on visiting in advance. While no one will expect you to be an expert on Day 1, it's always helpful to know the basics of a city before you make yourself at home.

Fortunately, the internet gives us access to a wide range of resources and information, so it's not difficult to jump online and do some digging around the local etiquette, taboos, and cuisine. **BBC World** (www.bbc.com/news/world/) is a great place to start and allows you to search by country, and to read up on international news. It even has a language learning section!

Another, no-tech way to learn about the culture you're in is to simply get out of your Airbnb or guest house and allow yourself to wander. Go to a local watering hole, grab a beer and observe. What are people ordering? How do they interact with each other? How do they touch each other, or do they avoid contact? You can learn a lot by spending some time observing.

Through observation, I've quickly learned how to get and pay for the bill in over a dozen countries and cities across the globe. In Paris, you wave down your server for the check then take it up to the cash register. In most Central American countries, you can raise your hand as if holding a pen, (ready to sign the check) and point it in the direction of your waiter. In Italy, the customs tend to vary, so I do as the locals do. Sometimes the entire transaction occurs at the table, other times it takes walking up to the counter and telling whoever makes eye contact with you what you ordered. "When in Rome," has never been more fitting!

CHAPTER 15

INTERACTING WITH THE LOCALS

While it can be difficult to remove ourselves from the comfort of the local nomad community—or perhaps from the pixelated virtual communities we engage with while abroad—it's important to break out of the bubble and experience the cities we're in through the eyes of the locals.

Couchsurfing has a great feature on their smartphone app called **Hangouts**. Update your availability with a quick "let's grab coffee" or "join me on a neighborhood walk" and locals and travelers in your current location will pop up. It's super easy to accept or decline a Hangout invite, and it's a fun way to connect with locals in your area. I used Hangouts when I was in Florence, Italy and made new friends from Croatia and Mexico, as well as meeting a very charming local who showed me the city's best cafes.

Don't forget to enjoy one of the main reasons you wanted to be a digital nomad in the first place—the freedom to experience new cultures. You may just surprise yourself by making lasting friendships or meeting your new startup co-founder.

HOW TO GIVE BACK

Living the digital nomad life usually finds us absorbed in our own projects, deadlines, and time-zone tracking. Our concept of reality and space can all but melt away, and spending 18 hours hunched over the computer can seemingly pass in mere minutes. But when we step outside of our own projects, and own adventures, some pretty incredible things can happen.

Finding volunteer work on the ground has a positive impact on the local community and on your experience there overall. I highly recommend checking out **WorkAway** (www.workaway.info), which facilitates volunteer and cultural exchanges in over 155 countries.

ANYWHERE

You can offer your tech knowledge to a local radio station in Reykjavik or learn organic farming skills in Phenom Penh. One of my favorite experiences from my recent travels found me in rural eastern England, running the daily operations of a large off-grid youth camp by day, and blogging by night. I don't think I've ever been more inspired for content than I was that month.

Another, simpler way to give back to your community is through mindful consumerism. Although not as glamorous-sounding as "international volunteer," you can still have a positive impact on the local economy by choosing to support local businesses when shopping for clothes, food, or any materials that help keep the digital dream alive. After your experience out in the community building relationships and investing in the local economy, you can return to your laptop and solve that major issue with your proposal, with newfound clarity and inspiration for your own projects.

With the freedom of living a digital nomad lifestyle comes a responsibility to be respectful of the communities in which we live, even if those stays are temporary by design. As you traverse the globe on your individual paths, keep in mind the communities around you that make such an experience possible. Be open to the stories of others, and give back in ways big and small.

CHAPTER 15

ABOUT THE AUTHOR

Emily Olson is desk jockey turned digital nomad. She works remotely for an awesome New York-based company, is an editorial intern for a travel magazine, and blogs occasionally about her travels. She is currently on a one-year world tour with her ten-year-old daughter. Spending the previous eight months volunteering and traveling through Europe, the duo are now enjoying less layers and more sun in Central America.

 @graveyardtravel

 @graveyardshifttravel

 www.graveyardshifttravel.com

Appendix:

SOS! EMERGENCY NUMBERS & RESOURCES FOR NOMADS

For U.S. Citizens: In case of emergency, the State Department recommends contacting the nearest U.S. Embassy or Consulate.

If you don't know where the nearest embassy or if you lost your passport, call Overseas Citizen Services:
1-888-407-4747 from the U.S./Canada
+1 202-501-4444 from overseas Travel Alerts & Warnings

The State Department also maintains a updated list of alerts and warnings. It's advisable to check www.travel.state.gov before venturing to a new city or country.

APPENDIX

MEDICAL EMERGENCIES WHILE ABROAD

To confirm the board certification of doctors abroad, visit www.certificationmatters.org or call toll-free at 1-866-ASK-ABMS (1-866-275-2267).

If you become ill or sustain an injury abroad, a consular officer from the U.S. embassy can assist in finding medical services and informing your loved ones back home. Please keep in mind that payment of hospital and other expenses is the patient's responsibility. You can learn more at usembassy.gov.

TROPICAL STORM SEASON GUIDE

Please bear in mind the following tropical storm seasons prior to planning travel:

North Atlantic: June - November
NW Pacific: July - November
NE Pacific: May - November
SW Pacific: October - May
South Indian: October - May
North Indian: April - December
(Source: US State Department)

SMART TRAVELER ENROLLMENT PROGRAM (STEP)

STEP is a free service that allows US citizens to make their nearest U.S. Embassy or Consulate aware of their contact information in case of emergencies. Consular officers at Embassies can help U.S. citizens who encounter serious legal, medical, or financial difficulties overseas. Create a free account at www.step.state.gov/step.

ANYWHERE

INFORMATION ON VACCINES AND OTHER HEALTH WATCH-OUTS

The Center for Disease Control and Prevention works to protect the United States from health, and safety and security threats from both at home and abroad. The CDC regularly updates their resources to provide helpful information about diseases and viruses abroad. The CDC will issue different types of notices for international travellers, for example:

- **Level 1** (Usual Precautions): Measles in Germany, Italy, Belgium & Indonesia.
- **Level 2** (Practice Enhanced Precautions): Zika Virus in Colombia, Bolivia, Puerto Rico & Fiji. Yellow Fever in Brazil.

Check for more travel notices and information at wwwnc.cdc.gov/travel. You can also search general health information by country via the **World Health Organization:** www.who.int/countries/en.

FINDING LEGAL HELP ABROAD

In the event you are arrested or face legal issues while abroad, you can request that prison authorities notify the U.S. Embassy or Consulate of the incident. The Consulate will provide a list of local attorneys who speak English, and can contact your loved ones and even your employer, with written permission. The Consulate can also share with you key information on the local criminal justice process. Note: The Consulate will not have the authority to get you out of jail or exempt you from legal action. Their role will be to provide the resources and context you need to determine appropriate next steps. In case of emergency, you can always contact your nearest U.S. Embassy or Consulate.

APPENDIX

CONTACTING CREDIT CARD COMPANIES ABROAD

Should you have issues with your banking provider or need to contact them while abroad, below is a list of numbers and resources to keep on hand.

American Express: Lists dozens of local numbers on its website www.americanexpress.com.

Bank of America: Dial the AT&T Direct Access Number of the country you're calling from followed by 302.738.5719.

Capital One: (Place collect call through operator first) +1 800-955-7070.

Chase: +1-713-262-1679

Citibank:

- **Latin America:** Argentina 08004448052, Brazil 08008911877, Other Countries +525522263988
- **Asia-Pacific Europe, Middle East and Africa:** +6565952255
- **Everywhere else:** 1-813-604-3000 (outside the U.S.)

Discover: +1-801-902-3100

Mastercard: Lists dozens of local numbers on its website, mastercard.com.

US Bank: +1-701-461-0346

USAA: 210-531-8722 or 800-531-8722

Visa: Lists dozens of local numbers on its website usa.visa.com.

WellsFargo: www.wellsfargo.com/help/international-access-codes

MISSING PERSONS

If you are concerned about a U.S. citizen, relative or friend who is traveling or living abroad, contact the US Embassy immediately at 1-888-407-4747. Information will then be provided to the Consulate abroad that will try to locate the individual and pass the message.

ANYWHERE

AND CO'S BIG LIST OF DIGITAL NOMAD RESOURCES

We referenced dozens of tools and resources in this book. Here's a list of all of them, with links for where you can learn more.

Resource	Description	URL
about.me	An easy-to-generate portfolio creator for freelancers to help present who you are and what you do.	www.about.me
Airbnb	Airbnb is a service that pairs digital nomads and other travelers with affordable housing around the world.	wwww.airbnb.com
AND CO	AND CO is the support system for freelancers. It's an app that helps digital nomads manage their businesses from proposal to payment.	www.and.co
AngelList	AngelList is a website for startups, angel investors, and job-seekers looking for a position at a startup.	www.angel.co
Apple Notes	Apple Notes is an application designed to record short text notes that is synched with all devices under Apple's iCloud service.	www.icloud.com/#notes
Asana	Asana is a project management tool that allows teams to collaborate over easy-to-use, intuitive lists. Its streamlined interface is perfect for remote teams.	www.asana.com
Auctor	Auctor pairs forward-thinking corporations with best-in-class independent creative talent. Auctor also offers curated remote work experiences for wanderlusting creatives.	www.auctor.com
Audible	Includes more than 215,000 audio books and programs for your listening pleasure that can also be downloaded for offline use.	www.audible.com
BBC World	BBC World is a news hub that allows digital nomads to conduct rudimentary research on current events at potential host cities and travel destinations.	www.bbc.com/news/world
Chiang Mai Buddy	Chiang Mai Buddy helps English-speaking nomads make Thailand their new home, whether the move is permanent or temporary.	www.chiangmaibuddy.com
ClassPass	A monthly fitness membership that allows you to visit different workout studios across the U.S. and in cities like London, Vancouver, Sydney, Melbourne, Brisbane and others.	www.classpass.com

APPENDIX

Couchsurfing	Couchsurfing connects nomads with locals who share their home and a global network of people.	www.couchsurfing.com
CoWoLi	CoWoLi is a service that supplies a list of living spaces to work around the world.	www.cowoli.com/coliving
Digital Nomads Forum	The Digital Nomad Forum is a community of 10,000+ nomads that ask questions and meet others around the world.	www.nomadforum.io
Domino	Domino is a search engine for finding great freelancers for your next project. They also offer a library of best practices for solopreneurs, called Domino Spot.	www.wearedomino.com
Dribbble	A show-and-tell for designers, Dribbble creates a platform for designers to share their work.	www.dribbble.com
Dropbox	Dropbox is a leading cloud-based storage solution.	www.dropbox.com
Evernote	Evernote is an app that serves as your digital file cabinet, note-taking tool, daily journal, task and project management system, and more.	www.evernote.com
Freelance Contract	The Freelance Contract is a templatized utility, co-developed by AND CO and the Freelancers Union, which allows digital nomads to easily create and execute secure work agreements with their clients.	www.and.co/the-freelance-contract
Freelancers Union	The Freelancers Union is the largest advocacy group for freelancers.	www.freelancersunion.org
Fulltime Nomad	A blog with tips on how to become a digital nomad to work and travel the world full-time.	www.fulltimenomad.com
GlassDoor	Glassdoor is a database of company reviews, salary reports, and interviews reviews and questions made by employees.	www.glassdoor.com
GlobeKick	GlobeKick is a three-month program that gives nomads the freedom to travel the world in a way that makes them more productive and successful.	www.globekick.com
Google Drive	Google Drive is a leading cloud-based storage solution.	www.google.com/drive
Google Translate	Google Translate is a service that translates text, speech, images, and videos from one language to another.	www.translate.google.com
Grammarly	Grammarly is an artificially intelligent grammar and spelling tool that helps digital nomads and other professionals ensure smooth and professional communication in spite of language barriers.	www.grammarly.com
Hangouts by Couchsurfing	Couchsurfing connects travelers with welcoming hosts around the world. Nomads can use it as an affordable housing solution.	www.couchsurfing.com/mobile-hangouts
Headspace	Meditation you can do when you want, wherever you are, in just ten minutes a day.	www.headspace.com
Hotel Tonight	Find discounted hotel accommodations up to seven days in advance.	www.hoteltonight.com

ANYWHERE

IFTTT	If This Then That (IFTTT) is an all-purpose automation tool that helps digital nomads automate a range of tasks by syncing actions that take place in separate apps with one another.	www.ifttt.com
Indeed	Indeed enables individuals to search for jobs that are posted on thousands of websites. It also enables you to apply to jobs with ease through an Indeed Resume.	www.indeed.com
Jobspresso	A database of remote jobs in tech, marketing, customer support and more.	www.jobspresso.co
Just Creative	Just Creative is a design portfolio and blog managed by Jacob Cass.	www.justcreative.com
Lexis Nexis	Lexis Nexis is an online academic database, available at academic institutions and public libraries, which allows digital nomads to research the local laws and tax stipulations of their host cities.	www.lexisnexis.com/en-us/gateway.page
Live & Invest Overseas	Live and Invest Overseas is a source for information on living, retiring and investing overseas.	www.liveandinvestoverseas.com
Locus Workspace	Locus is a coworking space that's based in Prague, an up-and-coming digital nomad hotspot in the Czech Republic.	www.locusworkspace.cz
Lonely Planet	Lonely Planet informs and inspires travelers and nomads with content from experts of each destination. The Lonely Planet app puts the breadth of their travel content in the palm of your hands.	www.lonelyplanet.com
Long Term Lettings	Listings for affordable long-term renting globally.	www.longtermlettings.com
Mangrove	Mangrove is a community of tech entrepreneurs, startup employees and freelancers who have and share the same ideals. Mangrove helps to grow as a group, and spread these values to communities.	www.mangrove.io
Mindful	Meditation made easy, via a simple app and associated blog.	www.mindful.org
My Local Crime	My Local Crime is a crime data aggregator that collects crime incidents and plots them on Google Maps. You can even sign up for alerts.	www.mylocalcrime.com
My Webspot	My Webspot allows nomads to rent pocket WiFi, access to high speed internet, everywhere around Europe at an affordable price.	www.my-webspot.com
N26	N26 is a mobile bank account throughout Europe for nomads. Money transfers are processed at the midmarket rate with no exchange rate markup.	www.n26.com/eu
Nomad House	Nomad House is a community that travels, works, and lives together in different parts of the world.	www.nomadhouse.io

APPENDIX

Nomad List	Nomad List finds you the best places in the world to live in and work remotely in. Joining Nomad List immerses you into a chat forum to meet other digital nomads.	www.nomadlist.io
NomadX	NomadX provides the infrastructure necessary for getting the remote worker away from the coffee shop, basement office or crowded co-working space and into a perspective-shifting setting, for as little as few days or as long as a few months.	www. nomadx.com
Numbeo	Numbeo is the world's largest database of information about cities and countries globally. Numbeo provides current data on world living conditions including cost of living, housing indicators, and traffic.	www.numbeo.com
Outsite	Outsite provides certain places around the world for people to stay, work and travel in.	www.outsite.com
Outsourcely	A platform for remote workers to find long-term, reliable jobs.	www.outsourcely.com
Pocket	Pocket helps you save articles, videos and more to a platform that is visible on a phone, computer or tablet.	www.getpocket.com
Quora	Quora is a Q&A based community that allows experts to answer questions fielded within the site. Users can upvote responses to surface the best for each query.	www.quora.com
Remote Work Hub	Remote Work Hub provides online courses for individuals and teams wanting to go remote.	www.remoteworkhub.com
Remote Year	Remote Year brings together 50 to 80 freelancers, nomads, and entrepreneurs on a year-long experience of working, traveling, and living in 12 different cities throughout the globe.	www.remoteyear.com
Remote.co	Remote.co is a resource for companies to hire remote workers and provides support to the organizations embracing the remote team as a significant part of their company.	www.remote.co
Remotely Awesome Jobs	A job post aggregator that focuses on consistently adding more remote jobs everyday specializing with employers who open directly to their site.	www.remotelyawesomejobs.com
Remotive	Remotive helps digital nomads to be more efficient by emailing them tips, running a community for support, and listing startups that are open to remote work.	www. remotive.io
ShareDesk	Sharedesk provides a platform for nomads to rent coworking spaces, business centers, or shared offices by hour, day, or month.	www.sharedesk.net
She Nomads	She Nomads is an inclusive environment for remote nomads in tech who want to travel. They provide free coding classes, study groups, book clubs, and more to their community members.	www.shenomads.com

ANYWHERE

Slack	Slack is a real-time collaboration tool that allows remote workers to easily navigate conversations with colleagues via group and one-to-one-chats, in addition to voice/video calls.	www.slack.com
Squarespace	Squarespace is a system that allows freelancers and businesses to create and maintain websites that have an impactful and user friendly online presence.	www.squarespace.com
StartupNation	StartupNation is a constantly refreshed resource for tactical guidance when it comes to launching and operating a small business or self-employed venture.	www.startupnation.com
Stowaway Cosmetics	Stowaway Cosmetics creates premium, cruelty free beauty products that are designed for travelers. The miniature products eliminate breakage due to travel, and reduce waste.	www.stowawaycosmetics.com
Sun and Co	Sun and Co is a place for freelancers and like-minded people to share a living and working space.	www.sun-and-co.com
The Gig List	Weekly email blast from AND CO, which curates and shares the top ten freelance and remote work opportunities in satirical fashion.	www.and.co/gig-list
The Life-Changing Magic of Tidying Up	Written by Marie Kondo, "The Life-Changing Magic of Tidying Up" presents a detailed manual about how to clear out clutter and live a more minimalistic lifestyle.	www.tidyingup.com
The Muse	The Muse is a resource that offers career advice from experts, and connections to get a private and personalized career coach.	www.themuse.com
The Remote Nomad	The Remote Nomad is a blog that shows nomads how to work and live anywhere. It includes online courses and a private Facebook group for nomads.	www.theremotenomad.com
Tortuga Backpacks	Tortuga creates sleek, utilitarian backpacks that help digital nomads navigate from place to place without the hassle of checking a bag.	www.tortugabackpacks.com
Trello	Trello is a colloboration tool that organizes projects into boards. It helps to easily see who is working on what project, and where something is in a process.	www.trello.com
Trusted Housesitters	Trusted Housesitters connect home and pet owners who need a sitter with trustworthy people who can sit for free.	www.trustedhousesitters.com
We-Roam	We-Roam is a program that creates travel itineraries from around the world for remote workers who want to travel without putting their careers on hold.	www.we-roam.com
WebWorkTravel	WebWorkTravel offers a destination guide for digital nomads with more than 60 affordable destinations from around the world.	www.webworktravel.com/travel-guide/
West Law	An app designed to have the most advanced legal research service for lawyers and legal professionals.	www.westlaw.com

APPENDIX

WeWorkRemotely	A job listing site for remote workers in different careers.	www.weworkremotely.com
Wifi Tribe	The Wifi Tribe is a group of people who live in different parts of the world together every month. They foster personal growth by coworking and coliving with each other.	www.wifitribe.co
Williams&Harricks	Williams&Harricks is a utility, developed by AND CO, that allows digital nomads to send physical demand letters to their late-paying clients.	www.and.co/williams-harricks
Workaway	Workaway is a resource that offers affordable accomodation in exchange for volunteering and working with local communities.	www.workaway.info
Workfrom	Workfrom is a user-curated list of thousands of workspaces around the world, from cafes and coffeeshops to coworking spaces and longer-term office venues.	www.workfrom.co
Working Nomads	Working Nomads constructs lists of the most interesting remote jobs in different professional fields.	www.workingnomads.co
Yonderwork	Yonderwork helps employers develop, implement and sustain a remote-friendly work culture.	www.yonderwork.com
Zapier	Zapier is a tool that allows you to connect apps you use every day to automate tasks and manage time.	www.zapier.com

Acknowledgments

We would like to thank the 100+ digital nomads and nomad experts who contributed to this book.

Contributing Authors:

Remi Alli, Simon Ammann, Lauren Alexander, Jessy Coulter, Joshua Hayford, Jennifer Miller & Tortuga Backpacks, Amanda Napitu, Ashley Nowicki, Emily K. Olson, Matt Prior, Aliya Rosenbloom & GlobeKick, Romina Viola

Additional Contributors:

Elizabeth Avery, Chris Backe, Leanne Beesley, James Cave, Katherine Conaway, Joseph Engelmajer, Sara Graham, Kelly Hayes-Raitt, James Hunt, Elijah Kelly, Ahmed Khalifa, Rose Lawless, Kelly Lewis, Janice Lintz, Peter Lovisek, Andrew Miller, Sarah Nourse, Ryan O'Connor, Monika Pietrowski, Josie Schneider, Alison Ward, Leigh Wetzel

Editors:

Katie Perry
Martin Strutz

Layout & Illustration:

Basia Grzybowska

Contributing Staffers:

Leif Abraham
Margarida Borges
Arielle Crane
Mario Gabriele
Hannah Le
Sharina Mirpuri
Guillermo Vasta

Thanks to all digital nomads who participated in AND CO's Slash Workers study (2017).

Created and Published by:
AND CO Ventures Inc.
www.and.co

© Copyright 2017. All rights reserved.

www.ingramcontent.com/pod-product-compliance
Lightning Source LLC
Chambersburg PA
CBHW040458240426
43665CB00039B/76